Endorsements for College Impact

Damian Boyd has created a catalytic resource in this book. It all at once inspires college students while challenging those who would lead them. Because of Damian's unique experiences, his persevering spirit and his unquenchable faith, this book will do more than teach. It will be an impartation.

J.D. Walt, Jr.
Dean of Chapel, Asbury Theological Seminary

I believe Damian's treatment of college students impacting their campuses is right on target. He is practical, and his concepts are easy to capture. Clearly, he has had first hand experience and is biblically trained in his approach. His work is not for students who simply want to "maintain" through their college years. But rather, it is for those who want to fulfill our Lord's Great Commission. I strongly recommend *College Impact*.

Richard B. Berry, Director of the African American Network
The Navigators

Many popular images of college life depict a time of carefree irresponsibility, pursuit of self-discovery, and quite often self-indulgence accompanied by music, laughter, and plenty of alcohol. Damian Boyd offers a much different vision for this strategic time of life. Rather than "checking out" of real life, *College Impact* challenges students to make the most of this time to make an impact on their campus and in the world beyond. Historically, college students have in fact brought about major changes in the world. Too many these days are content with much less. *College Impact* seeks to mobilize this generation of students with a much bigger vision that calls not just for "staying good," but moving out and making a difference for the cause of Christ. This is a great book for students and leaders who see the unique period called college as one of unprecedented opportunity for Kingdom good.

Evan Hunter, Director of the Ivy Jungle Network

COLLEGE IMPACT

Empowering Collegiate Christians
for Campus Influence

DAMIAN L. BOYD

Paramind Publications

PARAMIND PUBLICATIONS
A *Shift* in Thinking

ParaMind Publications

Copyright ©2009 by Damian L. Boyd

Published by ParaMind Publications, LLC
2090 Baker Road, Ste. 304-171, Kennesaw, Georgia 30144

Library of Congress Control Number: 2009912030

ISBN 978-0-9762738-2-0

Printed in the United States of America

www.paramindpublications.com

Acknowledgements

Thank you to all of the amazing leaders who have encouraged, taught, and inspired me over the years. Your words and lessons have not been in vain. To my wife Zarat, you are amazing and your encouragement and assistance has been invaluable. Kelli Caston, thank you for your help getting this book started. Inga Clark, your eye for detail is impeccable. Melissa Lawrence, I can't wait until the world discovers you; you are truly a treasure for the Kingdom of God. It's been a labor of love and you all have helped me so much. God bless you! Thank you to my pastor Dr. Bryan E. Crute, his wife Lanette. Destiny Metropolitan Worship Church family, I love you. Louie and Shelley and the Passion Movement, you're awesome!

Dedication

This is for my savior Jesus. Your grace is overwhelming, and I stand amazed at your Glory. I honor you with my life.

For my second love, my wife Zarat, you come next to Jesus alone. You are one of the best Christians and leaders I have ever met. You're a constant source of encouragement and support. You are simply the most amazing woman I have ever met. I love you.

TABLE OF CONTENTS

Foreword

I remember thirty years ago when I first began working with high school and college students. I sought out mentors—leaders who had experience; people who were effectively doing what I had started doing myself. They were few and far between. After four years, I drew some conclusions about effective student ministry. First, most were built around flashy events rather than quality discipleship and mentoring. Second, for every one effective ministry that equipped students to lead and serve, there were a hundred who merely entertained students each week with a program. Third, if we continue to do ministry to students the way most were doing it, we would never fully reach and impact our campuses for Christ.

In this book, you will read about a different model for doing ministry. It is based on the notion that leaders must equip and mentor students, not just shepherd them. Damian Boyd is convinced we cannot be satisfied with helping students survive college and remain true to their Christian faith. We cannot simply play defense. We must play offense, training them to initiate not react; to serve their fellow students on the campus not just attend meetings. In order to do this—we must disciple them. This cannot be done in massive groups, but through life on life mentoring relationships. I learned long ago that Jesus' philosophy for ministry enabled Him to fulfill his Heavenly

Father's will, but not become overwhelmed in the process. I believe Christ's philosophy for ministry went something like this:

- Love the whole world

- Minister to the many

- Mentor the few

I encourage you to not only read the thoughts in this book, but to practice them. Don't be afraid to adjust your present methods for ministry. Be counter cultural. In fact, I dare you to attempt to do ministry "Jesus style." You may be small at first. It may be slow growth at first. But eventually, you'll notice it will be real. And lasting. And it will multiply. Jesus said it would look much like a small seed planted in the ground. If you'll be patient, and not try to look like everyone else in student ministry, you'll one day be a model for others to follow.

May this book stir you to be different.

Dr. Tim Elmore
www.GrowingLeaders.com

Introduction

This book is intended to make college Christians dangerous: dangerous to the kingdom of darkness, dangerous to campuses closed to the gospel, and dangerous to all who name the name of Jesus but are unwilling to follow Him. It's time for those who love Jesus on the college campuses around the world to rise up and live for the glory of God alone. It's time to live in the marvelous freedom of the Son of God and embrace the life that has been painstakingly set before you as a follower of the King. It's time to be the people of God and impact campuses in desperate need of a Holy God.

As a college pastor, I have invested many years into students awakening to the greatness on the inside of them. It was my goal to lead a charge of students toward a loving savior. What I soon realized was that I could only do so much as a college pastor. It would take students to reach the people I would never come in contact with as a campus minister. We need more college pastors, for the purpose of challenging their students to impact the campuses. College students need strong leadership to both encourage and inspire them to live radical lives. Without it, students will, more often than not, fade into the background neglecting the charge of college influence.

The goal of this book is to help and encourage college believers to use their influence to impact their campuses for

Jesus. So, my prayer is that this book would ignite a spark that cannot be extinguished. May these simple words be used to help you figure out how you can have the greatest influence at your school. Its purpose is not only to inspire you, but also to give you the key strategies to leveraging your life for maximum influence.

THE CALL

College is an interesting time; it always has been. Think about it. You spend your whole life doing what you are told, following the rules (or rebelling against them, if you are like me), and trying to walk in the guidelines set for you. In high school, you were told where to go and how fast you should get there. You were supposed to do what you were told! This was best for you. It was all for your safety and well being. Thank God for parents and their restrictions, because without them, many would not make it to adulthood.

On the flip side, once you're in college, no one forces you to do anything. Don't want to go to class? OK. Want to sleep until 3pm? Go for it! You want to stay up and party all night and forego church? You're the boss! You are grown. Your parents are not there to hold your hand every moment of the day. You don't have to study, go to church, pray, read the Bible or do anything.

This reality hit me like a ton of bricks when I arrived at college. Someone dropped me off at my residence hall and drove off. I began to think, "I'm hungry." There was no one to drive me to the store. No one was there to point me to the kitchen for pre-purchased delicacies with which to stop my raging appetite. Once I found the cafeteria, no one told me not to make a pig of myself. I felt so alone and yet so free. If I walked away from God in that moment, who would care? Who would stop me? That's the college experience; it's a chance to either grow up or walk away from following Christ passionately.

For Christians, many take this as an opportunity to create a new identity and separate from the things that were "holding them back." Holding them back from experiencing what they would deem "fun." Sadly, that often means walking away from a vibrant relationship with Christ and anything that has to do with the Christian faith. The same wonderful youth group kids become total pagans by their senior year of college, others much sooner. Young believers are sometimes so hungry for worldly experiences, freedom from their parents, and freedom from the rigor of their faith that they gorge on the world and its poison kills them. Some statistics state the number of church kids that abandon the faith at over 80%. That is both a frightening and heartbreaking thought for the church at large. It means the next generation will potentially be lost.

Great Commission

My question is, "What happened to the Great Commission?" What happened to being light in a dark world? Jesus said...

"I have been given all authority in heaven and
on earth. Therefore, go and make disciples of all
the nations, baptizing them in the name of the
Father and the Son and the Holy Spirit. Teach
these new disciples to obey all the commands I
have given you."

Matthew 28:18–20 (NLT)

How will anyone come to Jesus if the ones who are supposed
to carry the message of love and hope give up? For all believers,
following Jesus should not be a fad or a thing to do. **It's a life of
reckless abandonment for the purposes of God in the face
of what the world presents.** This is the Great Commission:
to go and carry His name to the world and show others that
He is more beautiful and worth living for than anything else.
Now imagine the person who doesn't know God. The student
who didn't grow up in church or has never had a Jesus experience. Where and when would they have the opportunity to
hear about our great Savior? If most of the people who are there
to communicate the Good News to them are missing in action,
then there is a great need for more workers of God's Kingdom.

There are over 17,000,000 college students in the United
States. Around 80% of them don't profess to be Christians.
That means that college campuses are great mission fields. Many
young believers would give their right arm to be able to go to
some other country to lift a banner for Jesus. **But how many
will embrace the call to take Jesus to the campus nearest
them?** It's sometimes harder to make a difference in the place
you are most familiar. That's probably because the cost can be

much higher. When you go on a short term trip to another country, you have no reputation, no one knows you, and you will be leaving soon. On the campus, the situation is much different. Those people will see you every day and intensely inspect your life requiring you to live out the standards you profess. It will potentially cost you the life and the reputation that you have built for yourself. The truth of the matter is that this is the call for you to lay your life down, to deliver the most important message someone could ever hear so they can have an opportunity to live for Christ. That message should first be communicated right where you are.

Let's look at this critical message more closely. God created the universe, our planet, and us. He made us and wanted to enjoy a relationship with His creation. He gave us the greatest gift we could ever receive—Himself. A relationship with Someone who made everything, with His words... that's mind boggling! We ruined that connection with our sin. Sin is the one thing that God hates. Every person born since Adam and Eve was born with this terminal illness called sin. Sin, simply put, is deciding that anything or anyone is more important than following God and/or His instructions (we have all done that). That sin separates us from God and incurs His wrath. We were facing eternal death and separation from this amazing One.

Then God Himself came to earth to rescue us from this fate. Jesus came, born of a virgin, and lived a perfect life. He remained spotless so He could be a perfectly sinless replacement for the wrath we rightfully deserved. His death on the cross was in substitution for our sin. Jesus rose from the dead after three days, forever freeing us from our death sentence.

He did this ensuring that we would not perish, but have life eternal, with God who loves us as a perfect Father. Now, not only does death and sin no longer have a hold on us, but we can have an intimate relationship with Almighty God, who is more satisfying and enjoyable than anything else.

That is a ridiculous story, and it is completely true! What more could you ask for? Do you believe the story? Are you willing to risk your life on it? If not, then do you really carry the name Jesus? This is not to bring condemnation or guilt on anyone, but this is the basis of our faith. Before you can begin to influence your campus or anyone for Jesus, you must believe His story. Not only that, is it a story for which you are willing to die? Look at what Jesus said...

> "Don't think I've come to make life cozy. I've come to cut—make a sharp knife-cut between son and father, daughter and mother, bride and mother-in-law—cut through these cozy domestic arrangements and free you for God. Well-meaning family members can be your worst enemies. If you prefer father or mother over me, you don't deserve me. If you prefer son or daughter over me, you don't deserve me. If you don't go all the way with me, through thick and thin, you don't deserve me. If your first concern is to look after yourself, you'll never find yourself. But if you forget about yourself and look to me, you'll find both yourself and me."
>
> Matthew 10:34–39 (Message)

Jesus was not sharing His suggestions with us. This was the foundation for following Him. Tough, isn't it? Many people don't want to look at Jesus in that way. But God went through a lot to ransom us from hell, and He loves us enough to make sure that we are clear on what it means and should mean to us. **It's time to take the cross of Christ from being just an Easter story to a clarion call to discipleship.** These are the basics.

Count the Cost

You must decide who you are going to be. Will you be a part of the "falling away from the faith" crowd? Campuses are full of them. Or will you be a part of the "holding on to my faith" crowd? The latter are the people who only find the call of Christ important at church and at the local Christian fellowship. They are not looking to make any difference for Jesus on campus. They like safety over sacrifice. Or would you rather make sure you touch as many lives for Jesus as you possibly can before you leave the campus? These are the revolutionaries that this book is geared toward. It is also meant to awaken those who are asleep dreaming of this kind of impassioned life.

You must count the cost of discipleship. What will it potentially cost you if you really pour all you have into the cause of Christ? Popularity? Status? Your reputation? Take a moment to write out some of the costs in your life:

_____

_____

_____

These are what Jesus has always asked His followers to abandon. I am laying this point within the context of the college campus, but, honestly, this is the call for every believer. Will you answer? Can you crucify these things in your life so that real life might come forth?

Is Jesus worth more to you than anything in this world? That's the question that shows whether or not you are worthy of the name Christian. There are a lot of people who carry the title, but not all of them have answered the question. Some people, upon reading this, immediately think of areas of sin and struggle in their lives and wonder if I am referring to sin. Not directly. There are some who have a difficult time stepping beyond their challenges, yet they have still made the decision to follow Jesus at all costs. Others have the title Christian but refuse to give Him their all. You can't speak on the behalf of anyone else. God comes to each of us individually and asks, "Am I first? Am I most important? Am I more valuable to you than...?" We all must answer!

Step Up

Once you make the choice to follow Jesus, whatever the cost, you can begin to see the opportunities around you to display His name on the campus. God has set you up! Here is the principle: reach the campus, reach the world. If you can impact your campus for God's glory, you can reach any place. **Colleges are microcosms of society.** You have all of the major resources right around you. Whatever arena you want to reach ultimately, there is probably a type of it on or near your campus.

Let's look at a few examples. If your chosen field is…

Politics: There is an entire political system at your finger tips. It's called student government. Get involved! You may not like to run for office, but you may be able to work as an adviser for someone who does.

Business: Many of the student organizations have to run like businesses. Everything from bookkeeping to marketing, recruiting, and vision casting is happening around you everyday.

Media: Many schools have television and radio stations as well as newspapers. You can learn to communicate using the channel(s) the campus has already provided for you.

College is your proving ground. Not only will college afford you the opportunity to develop the skills to excel in your career, but it also will show you how to touch people who are within your skill set with the love of Christ. You can learn to impact people through your chosen field. Once again, reach the campus, reach the world.

Not only can you learn to reach the world while in college, you can also reach parts of the world through the students on your campus. How? Think about it! People from all over the world come to this country to study. You can reach a student who is from another country, and when they graduate they can then go back as a missionary to their own land. You can reach a culture you may never visit by impacting a person's life on your campus. The possibilities are endless. **Reach the campus, reach the world!**

Think about it. The next leaders of industry are sitting next to you in class. Future heads of state are in your study groups. The next multibillion dollar earner is right there. Imagine how that money could be used if you reached them with the message Christ has entrusted to you. Someone, whether for the better or the worse, will change the world in your generation. That could be you! Or it could be someone seated next to you. Will you be God's voice communicating His love?

God has not only set you up to shine your light to those within your future career. He has also given you a chance to touch the world. Are you beginning to see what God has placed before you for His Glory? You are in the perfect place to make potentially the largest impact of your life. Don't waste it. Yes, college is "supposed" to be fun. If you begin to live with an unquenchable passion for the Lord, you will see more excitement than you could ever imagine.

I had three roommates in college. One was American, one was Jamaican, and one was Liberian. I wish I could say they all came to the saving knowledge of Jesus because of my witness. But, my roommate from Liberia did come to the faith in school. He now is a minister and touches the lives of people that I will never meet in my lifetime. All of them have heard the good news. I was always nervous to tell them about my faith, but I realized that I may be the only person they ever met that who was bold enough to tell them the truth. Yes, it is scary to step out to tell someone about the love of God. It can be down right petrifying, but you will never know the effect of your evangelism efforts on the world.

A good number of collegiate Christians can't wait to tell the world about the God of love. As soon as they get out of college, they are going to charge into the world for the fame of God's name. The reality is that the world was at their footstep while they were in college. It's hard to realistically believe that we will change the world if we are not at least willing to change our campus. If God can trust you to invest your life into the 2,000 or maybe even 30,000 on your campus, He can trust you to reach a company, city, and maybe even a country. Jesus commended faithfulness in the small things through a parable. To a servant who starts small He says,

> "You are a good servant. You have been faithful in using a little. Now you will be leader over ten cities."
>
> Luke 19:17 (NLV)

God wants to use someone to make a difference for His name. Can God trust you to answer the call of leadership and service to your campus? Will you be the one God can use to shine your light for others to see Him? Will you reach the campus to reach the world? Will you leverage your life and your leadership to ensure people know about the love of a great God? This is the call that God is communicating to you. I encourage you to decide now if you're going to follow Christ in expanding His kingdom on your campus.

ALL IN

The greatest question the collegiate Christian has to answer is "Will I engage in the mission field of my campus for the cause of Christ?" If there is one person in your sphere of influence that does not know Jesus, then it's your job to give them the opportunity. As previously mentioned, the goal of this book is to help and encourage you as a college believer to use your influence to impact your campus for Jesus. But before we can discuss creative ways to evangelize, we must first go to the Father in prayer to prepare the way for a spiritual awakening. Hopefully, you have already discovered that there is a need to present or re-present the gospel on your campus. Now, make a decision to get in the game.

Vernon Johns, the Civil Rights Activist and former pastor of Dexter Avenue Baptist Church in Montgomery, Alabama (who was followed in his pastorship by Martin Luther King, Jr.) was once quoted as saying, "If you see a good fight, get in it." I love that quote. The premise is that there is always an opportunity to help fight an injustice or to bring light to an issue. We can always find a social issue in which to get involved. That is a great thing and should be applauded and encouraged. But, what about the more important issue of eternity? There is an Almighty God, requiring people to give their entire selves to Him. That supersedes all else. Everything we do should stem from that truth. That is the absolute best fight to get in.

It goes without saying that we live in a world that is very sensitive to violence, war, and aggression. In spite of that, we can't avoid the cold and hard fact that war, fighting, and struggle are a part of our spiritual legacy. The same God who loves and suffers long with His people is the same God who would send those same people into battle. You ask, "Haven't there been many wrong wars fought in God's name?" Yes, but that does not change the reality that we are still called to fight. The good news is that our battle is not with people; it's a spiritual one.

> "For we do not wrestle against flesh and blood, but against the rulers, against the authorities, against the cosmic powers over this present darkness, against the spiritual forces of evil in the heavenly places."
>
> Ephesians 6:12 (ESV)

The fight you should engage in is one for the souls of your classmates, professors, administrators, custodians, and future generations. The souls of the non-believing collegiate hearts are worth fighting for. How much do you pray for your campus? Are you willing to put in hard work for the sake of the gospel and the advancement of the Kingdom of God at your school? What are you willing to do?

This is not a challenge for the faint of heart. This is for those who see the desire of their Holy King and are willing to fulfill His plan to make His name great in all the earth. The life of campus leader is not an easy one. Many students think it's just enough to read your Bible and attend church. Some even go a step further and join a campus ministry so they can have their own group of Christian friends. All of these pursuits are very good, but they rarely result in the advancement of the good news, and by themselves bring no one into an intimate relationship with Jesus. Often, these exercises are the products of many whose efforts are to stay "saved" and avoid sinning. Simply put, it's playing it safe. The Bible is very clear on this matter:

> "Jesus said to His followers, "If anyone wants to be My follower, he must forget about himself. He must take up his cross and follow Me."
> Matthew 16:24 (NLV)

Take up pain, struggle, and discomfort for someone else's sake. It's not about us. If our lives are not buried in the life of Christ, then that says we don't have Him living in our hearts. Jesus gives us no provision for half hearted commitment. It's a Western gospel that causes us to have a "me-based" Christianity. But the reality is, it's about Christ and His plan in the earth, and it's that simple. Jesus tells us to go and be light in a dark world. **The student that lives uncomfortably for the sake of the cause of Christ will be the same one that does whatever it takes to glorify and magnify His name on his or her campus.** Is that you?

So what should your response be to a call from God to evangelize those around you? It should be, "I am all in, God! Whatever it takes!" Please know that nothing is by accident. You are on your campus for a reason. It's not just because you scored highly on a standardized test or because you received a scholarship. The moment you arrived at your school, there was hope for the souls of all who don't currently carry the name of Christ. Of course, you are there to get a degree and/or develop a skill set too. **What you don't want is to get an "A" in your coursework and an "F" in your Kingdom work!** This does not mean you must be a religion student or a philosophy major. Whatever your field of study, you should work hard to maximize your effectiveness both spiritually and educationally. When it comes to these two, it's not an either/or situation. It's a both/and. The spiritual and the natural side of a student are both necessary and are God-honoring for effective impact. We will explore this concept more later.

Morality vs. Christianity

Many college Christians focus only on the natural side of things and the result is a minimal effect on their campuses. The result is that believers look like everyone else. How can you tell the difference between a moral non-Christian and a Christian who will not stand up and out for Jesus? It's very difficult. Have you ever met someone and thought, "They must be a believer" and only later find out that they are not? Or have you ever talked to someone in class and thought 'they are not Christian' and run into them in your church the next week? It's good for these people to go to church, but please capture the principle.

We as believers have made Christianity equal to morality. Mormons are often moral people. Some Muslims are moral people. Some average everyday unbelievers have good home training and are very moral. Being a good person and being a good student does not make you a believer. A Christian's morality should confirm his/her belief system, not necessarily establish one. If morality established beliefs, then the Pharisees would have been applauded by Jesus because they had all of the outward religious signs. Pharisees were religious scholars with all of the outward signs of spiritual piety and little actual faith. But, on the contrary, He let them have it because their morality did not produce any spiritual awareness or understanding for most of them. They were so blind, in fact, that they were missing the one for whom they were searching. The Messiah was before them, but their "moral living" did not produce the result they thought it would. Ultimately, they sent the one they had been waiting for to His death. Here is the largest concern with the morality-based evangelistic approach. Good people don't go to heaven based on their goodness. You are not at school just to get a degree, but to make a difference. You are supposed to shine brightly!

Directly opposed to that mindset are two other groups of our friends—the flunking evangelists and the ultra-carnal Christians.

The flunking evangelist is someone who is always talking about Jesus and trying to lead people to Him, but they are on academic probation. This person will stay up all night writing a new worship song but won't go to class. These are amazing people with a lot of love for God; but they miss the fact that they are to worship God with their entire lives, including their grades. You avoid this downfall by focusing on classwork when necessary.

The ultra-carnal Christian is quick to tell people he/she is saved, but they live in a way that would embarrass both Jesus and his or her mother. These people have zero credibility and will not make a lasting difference. They have essentially disqualified themselves from significant leadership on campus. The remedy to this is to fully commit your life to Christ.

We will discuss how you can find a balance to these opposing lifestyles later, but the point is vital to the life of the collegiate Christian.

The concept is that you want to be all in, fully committed to making a difference for Jesus. Gambling is not generally a good analogy when writing a spiritual book, but please humor me and follow my train of thought. **When someone is going "all in," it means that they will put everything they have on the line.** Either they win it all or lose it all based on what they have in their hand. So it is for Christians. There is a risk in following Jesus. We don't always know where He will lead or what will happen. But, He is a risk that will never disappoint because in the end we win. Hallelujah! The journey will continually be revealed, but the path is in His hands. Going "all in" means you have chosen to take up your cross and follow Him, come what may. You will risk your reputation, your future, and maybe even your life. You are saying to God, "I will go wherever and do whatever you ask." Your only comfort is...

> For I know the plans I have for you, declares the LORD, plans for wholeness and not for evil, to give you a future and a hope.
>
> Jeremiah 29:11 (ESV)

Are you "all in?"

Have you made up your mind to give your all to God's Great Commission? Are you willing to do whatever it takes?

Write down a couple barriers keeping you from fully committing:

_____

_____

_____

_____

This is the question that will determine what kind of impact you will make. Don't expect a massive move of God on half-hearted commitment. How can God trust you with the great responsibility of campus-wide influence when you don't know if He is worth giving your whole life? Make no mistake about it: you are not "all in" until you are. There is no such thing as flaky full surrender to the plan of God. He and His call must be the most precious and worthwhile thing in your entire life for this to happen.

Tough Times

People who have this type of commitment look different. They have a special glare in their eyes. This only comes from people who have taken up their crosses. From people who have settled the death issue and determine that the cross is the type of death they want. For they are dead in Christ and they no longer live to themselves.

> "I have been crucified with Christ [in Him I have shared His crucifixion]; it is no longer I who live, but Christ (the Messiah) lives in me; and the life I now live in the body I live by faith in (by adherence to and reliance on and complete trust in) the Son of God, Who loved me and gave Himself up for me."
>
> Galatians 2:20 (Amplified Bible)

That's "all in." When we as believers live like this, we are not super-human or better than anyone else. We have simply made a decision to follow Jesus and have counted the cost and determined He is worth it. I am frequently asked a question from the students who are discovering this truth. That is, "Does it really take all of that?" The answer is yes! It takes everything you are, were, and will one day be.

This is the essence of worship—laying down our plans, hopes, dreams, and accolades that He may get the glory. Of

course, this may change the paradigm of many because we have
been conditioned to believe that worship is singing slow songs
about God. Worship is so much more than singing, although
singing is a part of a worship experience. Galatians 2:20 is
about worshiping God with our whole lives. That's the true
heart of worship.

Does your life speak of God in this way? Do people see the
glorious works of God in your actions? This kind of life is totally peculiar, different, and other. On the contrary, if this is
not at the core of our hearts then what does that say of the relationship we say we have with the Lord? If you haven't made up
your mind completely, you will faint when tough times come
and you will never risk anything for His cause. Our Western
culture seems to be missing the central Biblical understanding
that the walk of Christ is one racked with challenge, struggle,
persecution, and difficulty. We seemed to be so preoccupied
with this world's creature comforts that we miss the essential
spiritual truth. Look at the words of Jesus,

> "Remember the words I spoke to you: No
> servant is greater than His master...If they
> persecuted me, they will persecute you also."
> John 5:20, NIV

If Jesus said challenge would come to us, then you can be
assured that it will happen. I understand that this may not be
an easy concept to embrace or even think about. That does not
make it any less true. God loved Jesus and He still sent Him
to endure the hardship of the cross. Not so that we would be

exempt from rough times as some may advocate, but so we would be reconciled to the Father. It was not Jesus' ultimate goal that we be free from trouble and inconvenience. If that was the case then John 5:20 would be in direct conflict. It was His goal that in our embracing the life He gives we would see God's way as more desirable.

Jesus was not just a nice guy who is overly concerned with our earthly wants. Yes, God blesses and will continue to bless His people. But we are to rejoice in our blessing just as much as we do in our sufferings. Paul wrote,

> "I know what it is to be in need, and I know what it is to have plenty. I have learned the secret of being content in any and every situation, whether well fed or hungry, whether living in plenty or in want."
>
> Philippians 4:12 (NIV)

If Paul had to embrace hardship for the sake of Christ, what makes us think that we will have it any easier? Settle it. Tough times will come because you have chosen to walk with Jesus. Get over it! People may call you weird for taking a decidedly Christ-centered stance. Some may resent the fact that you believe in Jesus so much that you challenge their belief systems. Professors may pick on you because you choose to believe the Bible over their secular knowledge. It comes with the territory. When you are "all in" you are willing to put yourself in a potentially hostile situation to increase your reach as a Christian.

You may be asking yourself, "Wait a minute. I thought this was a book about college leadership?" You are correct. This is an encouragement that may keep you focused when someone challenges your stance. Not for you to become brash and arrogant. Certainly not to become so dogmatic that you chase people away before you ever get a chance to share this glorious good news. There are many practical elements to allow you to develop a strategy that will turn your campus on its ear. From Student Government to on-campus organizations, there are multiple opportunities to impact the campus. Without Christ as your driving passion, then all else is, at best, just gimmicks. It's that important.

There have been many to embark on the journey of campus impact, but when tough times came, they quit. Yes, with great zeal they purposed to launch out toward the total evangelization of their campus, and then when their roommates grew frustrated with them, they decided that the price was too high. If you catch the fire of God's love for your school and attempt to do something about it, you will receive persecution. Your roommate may not like you. The administration may not like someone boldly expressing their beliefs. Your professors will resent the snot-nosed student challenging their un-godly worldview. And yet this is still a worthwhile endeavor. It may be the hardest challenge you have ever experienced, but if God is for you, who then can be against you?

Whether you know it or not that is the beginning of leadership. It's all about looking at how you can leverage your life in such a way that people have the opportunity to follow you as you follow Christ. It should be your desire to be in the most strategic position to make the greatest difference. You want to be a voice for God. "All who are looking for life to the full come this way!" You want to be in the best place where you can get the most opportunities to get the greatest chance to communicate the greatest message.

A Question of Authority

Here is the other side of the equation: BIG GOD + tiny me = Glory for God. The focus is not and should never be the struggle itself. The focus should remain on the fact that the God of all creation will be with you. Before Jesus ascended into heaven, He gave the disciples (and we as believers) a huge charge.

> "Then Jesus came to them and said, "All authority in heaven and on earth has been given to me. Therefore go and make disciples of all nations, baptizing them in the name of the Father and of the Son and of the Holy Spirit, and teaching them to obey everything I have commanded you. And surely I am with you always, to the very end of the age.""
>
> Matthew 28:18–20 (NIV)

Wow, that is a scary thing for 11 guys (of course Judas had hung himself by then) to have to accomplish. He literally placed the goal of reaching the entire world in the hands of 11 people. Either Jesus was crazy or it was absolutely possible. The beginning of this scripture gives us the key components to see this monumental task come into being. In verse 18, Jesus came to them and said, "All authority in heaven an on earth has been given to me..." Then He hits them with the THEREFORE. "...Because I have all power, therefore go." Can you hear the disciples saying to themselves, "Oh, great Jesus. It's nice that you came with all power, but you are about to go away." Now He gives them the critical part that would ensure that the goal is accomplished. "I will be with you always, to the very end of the age." Not only does He have all authority, power, and rights, but He will be with us. That is good news!

This means that everything you need to fulfill the great commission on your campus is in you right now, if you name the name of Christ. You are not ill-equipped to accomplish this goal. As a matter of fact, you have more than you need. This is an exciting thought and an even more awe-inspiring reality. We truly can do all things through Him who gives us strength as Paul continues in his explanation of his "struggle" in Philippians 4:13.

Gut-check Time:
Do you believe that God can do anything through you, and in spite of you?

If you don't believe it, you will never step out to try anything great on your campus. Your belief in the fact that God is in, with, and wanting to empower you is proven one way: you have to live like it. This belief requires action. It is not enough to just mentally ascend to this. People who walk with the awareness that God is with them leave a wake behind that has the distinct marks of God's present existence.

Take a moment to think. With God moving through you, what can you accomplish? The possibilities are endless! The reason more of that amazing stuff that you could, maybe should be doing with God's empowering is not happening is not God's problem. His arm is not too short to save. The problem is you; the very people who claim to carry Him. **We trade the truth of God for a lie by deciding that the pleasures of this world are more important than fulfilling His great commission.** Or we live at such low moral levels that we would embarrass Him to a point that He doesn't do anything great through us. A little more painful, is that we know He is with us, but we refuse to move into what He has for us.

So, what do we do? Peter is a good example of what our response should be.

> "During the fourth watch of the night Jesus went out to them, walking on the lake. When the disciples saw him walking on the lake, they were terrified. "It's a ghost," they said, and cried out in fear. But Jesus immediately said to them: "Take courage! It is I. Don't be afraid." "Lord, if it's you," Peter replied, "tell me to come to you on the water." "Come," he said. Then Peter got down out of the boat, walked on the water and came toward Jesus."
>
> Matthew 14:25–29 (NIV)

When Peter saw Jesus on the water, it settled the question of power that Jesus possessed. He did not just want to watch this glorious act; he needed to be a part of the story. When Peter asked to come out on the water, he discovered a few things. First, if God bids you come, you can do the impossible. Second, you must keep your eyes on He who is calling. Third, when you stumble and fall, God can pick you up.

You will find the same thing if you choose to step out on the proverbial waters and do a work on your campus for Jesus. If you see His miraculous life and decide to test the waters of out-loud living, then you might just be able to do something great. Imagine what that would look like. If you keep your eyes on Him and continue to walk on the proverbial waters of your own campus, how glorious would that look to the unbelievers who are looking for more purpose, more joy, and more life? Here is the good news: in moments when we take our eyes off of Him, His grace is always extended towards us to pick us up so that we can continue on this journey. Now do you see how possible it is for God to win an entire campus for Himself? What then will be impossible? Even if you falter, God will pick you up and help you along because you took a risk in His name.

Caution: Make sure you don't do one of the worst things possible. That is to say, "Yeah, Jesus, let's take the campus," and use this as an excuse to be obnoxious.

God is love. He sent Jesus to earth to die because of His love. It is our responsibility to share the message and live the life that supports our verbiage. It is, not nor will it ever be our job to force anyone to hear us or use our faith to hurt people. We are to give people the opportunity to yield to the truth that there is one way to the Father – that is through Jesus the Christ. If someone does not want to embrace this, then we are to pray for them and move on. Some Christians have taken it on themselves to demean and demoralize those who do not believe. We would not have yielded to the good news if someone would have put us down and/or made us feel like they were better than us. The difference between a believer and an unbeliever is forgiveness. We are to reach out and love hard at the same time. This is how we can reach this very sensitive generation that rarely responds favorably to the wrong approach.

Caution: To the timid, some believers rely solely by the philosophy of "I will just let my light shine through my life." Although, this is a good thought, the reality usually differs quite a bit.

It usually means I will play it safe and fly under the radar as to not bring attention to myself. Then by some miracle people will just flock to me because I am a Christian. That is the exact opposite from letting one's light shine because the very nature of light is that it eliminates and expels darkness.

> "Neither do people light a lamp and put it
> under a bowl. Instead they put it on its stand,
> and it gives light to everyone in the house."
>
> Matthew 5:15 (NIV)

Light will attract attention; Jesus brought attention because of who He was and what He was doing. Just try containing light. It seeps into every crevasse possible. It's invasive, not passive! Some people are very comfortable in the background. That is perfectly fine. The key is to make sure that your voice has reach. This will even bring moments of attention to the shyest of people. When this happens you can still convey God's love in your own way.

We are a part of the New Testament church. The great commission has no expiration date. We are to take the message of Jesus to the world. There is an awesome opportunity for college students to touch lives for Jesus. Please don't waste one moment God has given you. You have the option to see your collegiate experience as an assignment or as just circumstance. What will be said of your time in school? Will you fail in your spiritual commitment? Yes, life with its trappings is calling you. Yes, you should enjoy your college experience! Yes, you are a student and must graduate. But, you should be a believer first and magnify Christ as a loudly and as strategically as you can. **The question is, "Will it matter that you were at your school at all?"** You have to answer that question.

PRAYER PRINCIPLE

Before you launch out with some grand scheme to reach your campus, it's important that you first have a real prayer focus. **Prayer should always precede your proclamation, processes, people, programs, and it will lead in all progress.** That's the prayer principle! Here are some common sayings about prayer that I have heard a million times, *"You should pray there before you go there and Prayer changes things."* They are both true! We have an audience with the Creator. That is an amazing thing to consider. Take a moment to think about that. All Mighty God wants to hear your prayers. James 5:16 tells us, "The prayer of a righteous man is powerful and effective."

Prayer is both a privilege and responsibility of a believer in which we are expected to participate. It's not simply a suggestion nor is it just a great idea. It's an expectation from God. In the book of Matthew, Jesus gives us a glimpse into His perspective and the necessity of prayer. Pay close attention to Jesus when He says, "when you pray."

> "And *when you pray*, do not be like the hypocrites, for they love to pray standing in the synagogues and on the street corners to be seen by men. I tell you the truth, they have received their reward in full. But *when you pray*, go into your room, close the door and pray to your Father, who is unseen. Then your Father, who sees what is done in secret, will reward you. And *when you pray*, do not keep on babbling like pagans, for they think they will be heard because of their many words. Do not be like them, for your Father knows what you need before you ask him."
>
> Matthew 6:5–8 (NIV)

These three words hold a monumental truth. We should pray! This is not an, if you pray, it's a when you pray. The overarching principle Jesus is sharing in this scripture is how to pray effectively. But constant prayer is implied. This is important as you prepare the way for a move of God for those with whom you will interact at school.

Praying in Secret

One of the greatest things you can do is pray for your campus. Some of our more outgoing brothers and sisters try to make prayer an opportunity to be loud and obnoxious to show their spirituality. Jesus encourages us to pray in secret and says that God will reward us. It's the secret prayer for your roommate, classmates, and campus ministries that will yield some of the greatest effects. Have you considered having strategic times of prayer when everyone else on campus is focused on other things? This is when your true spiritual life shows up, when you are laboring for the God-kind of results in private.

You have to consider the freak-out factor when an unbeliever overhears your prayers. Imagine the look of a non-Christian's face as his/her Christian roommate is praying at the top of their lungs, "Save them, God. They are such sinners. They are going to HELL. Allow them to see how dirty their lives are, in Jesus' name. I love you. Amen." Do you think that unbelieving roommate will then turn over and say to themselves, "I am so glad they pray for me?" No, they are going to the housing office in the morning to request a roommate that is not crazy. Get me an Atheist, a Satanist. Even a weird guy who cures his own meat in his room will do… just not the crazy Christian! Secret prayer is a very powerful thing. Toward the end of the chapter, there will be some strategic prayer focuses that may help you in your campus focused prayers.

This is not saying that you should pray any less because you don't want to embarrass yourself. No, pray. Pray hard! Pray and believe that God hears you most clearly. Sometimes we can try to save people *by* our prayers and not touch God *with* our prayers. The difference is that we shouldn't beat people over the head with prayer. Rather we should seek to touch the heart of God on their behalf. We get no credit for what people hear, only that which God hears.

Prayer Is Spiritual

The Bible is very clear about the fact that we are not just dealing with natural beings and situations. We are fighting, wrestling, and contending for the very souls of men and women. This is not an over-spiritualization of a simple premise; it's the naked truth. There is a real spiritual world, a real God, real angels, real demons, and a real devil. That's why we must know and accept this call to pray. It's just as, if not more important than, the outward ways we wish to make a difference. Here is the key: before you go there, pray there.

Please don't underestimate the power of your prayers to God. The Bible says, "The prayer of a righteous man is powerful and effective."

> "...The earnest (heartfelt, continued) prayer of a righteous man makes tremendous power available [dynamic in its working]."
> James 5:16 (Amplified Bible)

Often many Christian students neglect prayer for different reasons. But, you can't afford to be missing in prayer. Let's look at a few reasons why Christian students don't pray.

Some think that...

1. God does not hear their prayers.
2. God does not want our little prayers.
3. God won't answer our prayers.
4. My prayers will not make any difference.
5. My life is too messed up to pray.

All of the above feelings about prayer are both normal and common. Confronting these thoughts is the key in praying prayers that make a difference. The Bible says ...

> "...If my people who are called by my name will humble themselves and pray and seek my face and turn from their wicked ways, I will hear from heaven and will forgive their sins and restore their land."
>
> 2 Chronicles 7:14 (NLT)

Let's take some time and extract some principles from this scripture.

The scripture in context finds Solomon at the completion of the temple of the Lord when God appears to him. God says to Solomon that He has heard the prayers, and that when some bad things start happening this is what you do. Then, He lays on Solomon the "if my people" line, which is where we park ourselves if we follow Jesus. "If My people, who are called by My name..." Simplified, My people who carry My Name. The connection again for us is that we are God's people!

Since you have Jesus' name on you, you know you're called a CHRISTian (little Christ). This is a starting point. You have an opportunity to talk to and know that God wants to hear from you because you are one of His people. This is the privilege that we have as believers; we have an audience with Almighty God. Really, think about that reality a little. The Creator of the Universe wants to hear from you. Wow! It is almost unfathomable.

The second mind-blowing part of this scripture is "will humble themselves and pray." Once again this is a portion of this scripture with massive implication for the Christian heart. To be humble is to both realize and embrace one's own depravity and fallibility. We are in a culture that is self-seeking and self-reliant. Not many people are willing to admit their own weakness and lack. We are often trying to make a name for ourselves or to become someone great and someone that others look up to and admire. That, in itself, is not bad. But often we are led to think that it means we have it all together. For example, in our celebrity culture, celebrities are made to look flawless and are often above even the law. When someone is exposed to be less than what their "image" is, then people are shocked as if the person was perfect from the beginning.

Humility says that we are human, and we need someone larger and better than ourselves to accomplish our life's passions and purposes, namely God. It also says that man can't live alone. We need others to help us come into that great place God has for us. No one comes to greatness alone. We all get and need help, and at times, we need to ask for it! Becoming a person of status is not bad! It's when we forget God and others and think we are more than we actually are that gets us into trouble. Make no mistake. The Bible says "God opposes the proud but gives graces to the humble." James 4:6 (NLT)

God is literally against the prideful. So to humble ourselves is of the utmost importance. Humility lies in your willingness to admit the truth: that you have no power or authority to make any difference apart from Christ. Humble yourself! We need to pray because the job of impacting your campus for Christ is larger than you can accomplish in your own strength anyway. There is no room for pride when you have to ask Perfection for help.

Prayer is communication with God, simply put. Humility and prayer are directly connected because when you realize that you don't have the power to change people then all you have is God. Think about it. At people's lowest moments, they are usually left with a very telling statement. "Oh, my God!" We hear this prayer when people go through their roughest times. When we are almost immediately aware that we are powerless to do something, we hear it. Then people lean on God, but when things get better, the same heart is not kept. Dependence shifts back to the individual and communication with God is no longer needed. It's when we continue the conversation after tough times that our prayer lives are established.

Pray and Seek

Then we are to open mouths and hearts and pray. "Seek my face," is what God says. This has everything to do with intentional search and pursuit. We can think of prayer as a passive thing, but prayer takes activity. Think about when you were a child and were playing hide and go seek. You could not stay still and expect others to come to you. When you are "it," you are required to aggressively pursue others. This is the same type of impassioned prayer we should have. The Bible clearly shows that God hides his face in times of rebellion and overwhelming sin. "With a little wrath I hid My face from you for a moment." Isaiah 54:8 (NKJV) When we seek God, we are not only looking for Him, we have to move, search, follow Him to the end that we are where He is. Just like when you were a child. Make no mistake about it. Some of our campuses are in gross sin or have moved away from a spiritual foundation like many Christian schools, Ivy League institutions, and historically Black colleges and universities. Where there is no visible sense of the presence of God, someone must be willing to pray in an intense pursuit of a Holy God to ask for God's favor and presence to realign us and set right what is wrong.

We have a role to play. Maybe your campus has never had any type of Christian presence. If that is the case, then thank God you are there. The question that comes next is, will you be moved in your heart to find God in the midst of a campus that has a culture in which He is not even a consideration? Will you intensely pursue the one who can make the difference? **"Will you be the one who will seek God for a change and ask for His tangible presence on your campus?"**

Turning

The next statement in this scripture is what trips many people up. "Turn from your wicked ways." This sounds so condemning, especially when we are wrestling with guilt from some sin we've recently committed. To get the true heart of this concept, we need only look at the New Testament equivalent. It's called repentance. Turning from the sin in which you have sullied yourself. It's a 180 degree turn away from our own sin. That should never be guilt inducing, but rather grace enhancing. It's God's wonderful goodness that even makes us want to repent. We should be filled with gratefulness that we are loved by God and He is drawing us to turn from the ways that lead to death. It's a wonderful thing.

Before you can turn from your wicked ways you must recognize your own wickedness. This is not an exercise in self-loathing, but it is the naked truth about our lives. There are always areas that we need to work on and change. You know those sin areas or places in your life where you are horrible example of righteousness. Why is your personal life important to make a difference on your campus? Who will God be able to set as an example of how to live if you aren't pure before God? If the ones who are praying are not clean before Him, what does that speak of the quality of the pursuit? If we look just like those who don't know God, then what are they to think about this God who we say is Holy? Your willingness to change and be changed displays how sincere you are and how prepared you are for God to reveal Himself on your campus.

When we do all this, He comes and heals the land. Those broken, sinful, dark, campus grounds many of us walk on everyday can be healed by the grace of God exploding in the lives of students, faculty, and staff. That is one way that you can bring a God kind of transformation on your campus. You should be the prayer warrior for your campus. The Bible says

"IF" my people, that means that we have to choose to pray. You can't be missing in action when it comes to specific and intentional prayer for your school.

When we do these things—humble ourselves, pray, seek His face, and turn from our sin—God says that He will hear our prayer, forgive our sin and heal our land. To think that God could actually do something great on our campuses is an amazing thought. Does your heart burn within your chest at the thought that God could save your room or suite mate? Do you believe that God wants to come to your campus in such a way that someone would choose to keep their virginity tonight? Someone may choose to no longer binge drink because God is present. Or even better, that a Christian will come alive to the Gospel of Jesus Christ and leave their safety zone and dare to share their faith with others. And maybe, just maybe, someone will lay down the lives they deem so precious and take up the cross of Christ and follow him. In what better work is there to be engaged? This puts a premium on your prayers, humility, diligence, and brokenness. Who will, for Christ's sake, pray and humble themselves for His cause?

Just Talk and Listen

Here is an easy step. Just talk to God about everything that concerns you. As Christians there is no growing out of that. Every person used significantly by God talks with Him. It's a simple thing, but just talking gets the dialogue moving. Don't try to pray like someone else. They pray that way for many different reasons. God wants to hear your voice and through your personality. Just talk. And allow God to speak to you.

Now that can be a scary and different thought. We look at God speaking to people in scripture, and we often don't have a clue of how to hear from Him. Be assured God speaks to us.

> "For God [does reveal His will; He] speaks not only once, but more than once, even though men do not regard it."
>
> Job 33:14 (Amplified Bible)

God is always speaking; we have a hard time listening. It's not usually considered a conversation with God because when He speaks it is called revelation (revealed knowledge). If it helps you to feel more comfortable talking to God or hearing from God, then I see no major issue with thinking about prayer as merely a conversation. Just know in your heart that you are communicating with the most amazing being that ever has and ever will exist.

Some may say that you should hear God audibly. Others say it's a feeling in your heart. And others say it's a thought in your head. There is proof of all three happening in scripture. Here is one way that God will always speak to you: through the pages of the Bible. If you want to know what God is saying, read the Bible. Even if people think or believe God spoke to them in another way, it always should be confirmed with the 66 books of the Bible. That is where the proverbial rubber meets the road. If you want to know what God has said and is saying, go to the very Word of God and read and listen.

I'm a little skeptical of people who always say that God is speaking to them. Not that God doesn't speak for He truly does, but some try to use God as a tool by which they can get what they want. If they say, "God said...," then people are prone to listen without thinking through what they say critically. I first want to know if what "God is saying" is biblical. God will never contradict His word. Then, I want see the fruit of the fact that God speaks to them in their lives. There should be some evidence that God is speaking to and through them. I have heard people say God told them to sleep with someone who was not their spouse. Ridiculous! That is in exact opposition to what the Bible teaches about sex. But, that is why we need to allow the Word of God to be out most important guide.

Fast to Fast

Fasting is a bad word to a Western culture. We often live such lives of privilege that we don't know what it is to deny ourselves life's pleasures for God's purposes. When we see prayer in scripture it is frequently followed by fasting. In the Bible we see a great example of what happens when prayer and fasting are coupled together. The book of Mark teaches us what Jesus says about the two when combined.

> "Then one of the crowd answered and said, "Teacher, I brought You my son, who has a mute spirit. And wherever it seizes him, it throws him down; he foams at the mouth, gnashes his teeth, and becomes rigid. So I spoke to Your disciples, that they should cast it out, but they could not." He answered him and said, "O faithless generation, how long shall I be with you? How

long shall I bear with you? Bring him to Me...
When Jesus saw that the people came running
together, He rebuked the unclean spirit, saying
to it, "Deaf and dumb spirit, I command you,
come out of him and enter him no more!"
Then *the spirit* cried out, convulsed him greatly,
and came out of him... And when He had
come into the house, His disciples asked Him
privately, "Why could we not cast it out?" So
He said to them, "This kind can come out by
nothing but prayer and fasting."

                              Mark 9:17–29 (NKJV)

The disciples had been given the authority to cast out
demons. Have you ever tried that? It's scary stuff. Most people
don't even know what that is like, but even with that authority
they could not cast this demon out. Then, Jesus cast out the
demon from the child and said something remarkable: "This
kind can come out by nothing but prayer and fasting." Isn't
that amazing? No matter how much power we think we have,
some great oppositions from the enemy will not be removed
until accompanied by our fasting and prayer. It's not a question
of salvation, but that of preparation and power. Jesus said some
things would take our increased commitment. We have our
part to play in God's work.

It is also important to note that Jesus himself had to both
fast and pray. So what is fasting? Fasting is self-denial for the
sake of spiritual increase. Whether casting out demons like
Jesus or changing the heart of a leader for God's sake (Esther

and Nehemiah are great examples of that) or praying for an answer like Daniel did, fasting is key.

Fasting is usually related to limiting eating because this is one natural desire that we can control. This is a good practice, and it prepares you to handle the major spiritual challenges that you will face on your campus. Can God trust you to turn over your plate? There are others ways to deny yourself, especially if you have dietary restrictions. Will you cut off your TV, radio, or the Internet for the betterment of His kingdom? Fasting is not fun, but it is necessary. Fasting and prayer together can open many doors that you can't on your own.

One way to start fasting is to spend one meal fasting and spending that time reading the Bible and praying for your campus. Don't eat any food for one meal for one day. Commit 30 minutes to an hour to God for the purpose of His name being made known on your campus. After developing that discipline move to two meals and upward toward an entire day and beyond. Please remember that your body is probably not used to this type of denial, and it will not feel good. But know that the benefits are immeasurable. You will not die from missing a meal or two or even going days without food. People can fast for up to about forty days without any long term physical effects.

Caution: If you have any health concerns like diabetes, hypertension, Crohn's disease, etc., you should contact your physician first. If you are restricted from a food fast, then you may want to find another thing you can fast from like entertainment.

If you are familiar with fasting, then you may want to find a way to increase your fasting and prayer times. It has nothing to do with the amount of time spent fasting and praying but rather amount of sacrifice in your life. Some think much of themselves and think they are more spiritual because of the amount of fasting and praying they do, and that is the wrong heart. Fasting should decrease you and your perspective and increase God and His perspective. Isaiah 58:1–9 gives great guidance in this area.

> "Shout! A full-throated shout! Hold nothing back—a trumpet-blast shout! Tell my people what's wrong with their lives, face my family Jacob with their sins! They're busy, busy, busy at worship, and love studying all about me. To all appearances they're a nation of right-living people—law-abiding, God-honoring. They ask me, 'What's the right thing to do?' and love having me on their side. But they also complain, 'Why do we fast and you don't look our way? Why do we humble ourselves and you don't even notice?'
>
> Well, here's why: The bottom line on your 'fast days' is profit. You drive your employees much too hard. You fast, but at the same time you bicker and fight. You fast, but you swing a mean fist. The kind of fasting you do won't get your prayers off the ground. Do you think this

is the kind of fast day I'm after: a day to show off humility? To put on a pious long face and parade around solemnly in black? Do you call that fasting, a fast day that I, God, would like?

This is the kind of fast day I'm after: to break the chains of injustice, get rid of exploitation in the workplace, free the oppressed, cancel debts. What I'm interested in seeing you do is: sharing your food with the hungry, inviting the homeless poor into your homes, putting clothes on the shivering ill-clad, being available to your own families. Do this and the lights will turn on, and your lives will turn around at once. Your righteousness will pave your way. The God of glory will secure your passage. Then when you pray, God will answer. You'll call out for help and I'll say, 'Here I am.'

(Message)

We fast so that God can be evermore glorified through our lives. We fast so that God can use us to enhance the lives of those who are in need around us. Jesus made the life of the demon possessed girl better through His fasting. So there should be no prayer and fasting deficits in our lives. We all must come before God for His magnification in our lives and in the world, to the end that your campus might be a place where God's presence is felt and recognized.

Who should you pray for?

Pray for your Leadership:

- Pray for the Administration—Pray that they would have encounters with God and would make decisions that would ultimately glorify God.

- Pray for your Professors—Pray that they would come to know Christ intimately and teach the information you need effectively.

- Pray for your Student Government—Pray that God would lead them in a way that honors Him. Pray that they would use their influence for Him.

- Pray for your Residents—Pray for those who live in your dorm, hall, or apartment building. Ask God to give you words to encourage and reach out to them.

- Pray for your Residential Hall Director—Pray that they would create an environment that allows you to live in peace and close community with others.

- Pray for your Resident Assistants—Pray that they would be examples of upstanding living.

- Pray for those who clean your hall—Pray for their families; pray for their encouragement.

- Pray that your entire campus community will come to the saving knowledge of the son of God!

And there are other prayers:

- Pray for those in your classrooms. Pray that they would meet Jesus personally and would excel academically.

- Pray for the Christian Organizations. Pray that they would be effective in reaching people for Jesus.

- Pray against any major strongholds on your campus: drunkenness, cheating, corruption, depression, fornication, etc.

- Pray for the surrounding community

- Pray for future students

- Pray for a spiritual Awakening

There are always reasons to pray!

Fasting Suggestions

- Find one spiritually mature person to be accountable to in the area of fasting.

- Start by fasting one meal.

- Weekly increase the amount of meals you will skip.

- Devote the time typically spent eating to prayer and Bible reading.

- Set prayer focuses during your fasting time.

- Shut off entertainment mediums during your times of fasting.

- As you grow in your ability to fast, set fasting time limits; for instance, one day fast, three day fast, seven day fast, etc.

HEART CHECK

When considering your campus and God's heart for it, you must find your area of giftedness and calling. This is where many miss the mark on campus. When we lack specificity and clarity, we lack effectiveness. Yes, we are supposed to reach the world through our message, but we all have a unique way in which we go about it. Jesus calls us to be fishers of men, and as fishermen and women we must decide what it is we are trying to catch. How you fish determines what fish you will catch? You don't catch a marlin the way you catch a catfish. It's up to you to prayerfully examine your gifts, passionate areas, experiences, abilities, and style. Each one of these areas are a guide in showing you where you will be most effective. Not every unbeliever will respond to a Bible study in the middle of the day in the center of campus. Some might, but if that is what you are to do, then you must find those would be drawn to that type of activity. This is not an easy process, but it could save you a lot of unnecessary energy and time. On average, you will have between four and six years to make your mark on your campus. So it would behoove you to be as strategic as possible.

Before we discuss your heart's desires and plans, it's important to assess the needs of the campus. If you focus on what you would like to do for God on your campus without taking some inventory as to the needs of your campus that is inconsiderate at best. Some things are easy to determine. If you are an athlete and you have a heart for athletes, then it may not be hard to assess their concerns. For a grad student who has a heart for first year students, it may be a little more difficult. This person may need to look at what grabs their attention, what they listen to, and what first year students desire. All these answers could change from situation to situation. Take some time and write down at least three areas of great need on your campus:

_____

_____

_____

_____

One key is to try to do some research on the population in which you are interested.

It's all about strategy. You must marry your heart with the needs of those who you want to touch with God's love. When you can connect the interest of your target group and your personal heart desires that can produce some amazing results. You have a short time to reach people on your campus and the surrounding community. You should want to maximize every moment.

Gifted

You are gifted. You have received gifts by both God and your parents. Some things you were born with and you're good at them. You have some areas in your life where you are exceptional... so much so that even when you fall short or don't do your best you still blow people away. Even while you are reading this book, one or two things probably sprung up in your heart. But, some are saying, "No, not me." If you are having a hard time believing that you are gifted, then let's examine that further. You have an area of exceptional ability whether you know it or not. What is the root of some people's feelings of inability? Could it be an esteem issue? It may surprise you that a lot of people struggle with believing that there is something extra special inside of them. We must learn to accept and believe that we are exceptional in some area! It is not subject to how confident you are in that particular area. It's inside of us regardless. Others don't think they are gifted because they are untested in an area. The gift is still there. The challenge in these instances is to try to take some risks in order to discover your untapped abilities. Risks will often reveal your zones of exceptional ability.

Then there are those who don't know their area of giftedness because they have never seen it. You are great in some area whether or not you have seen it. For example; your place of giftedness may be golf, although you may have never played it to know it. Or you may not have had the means to play, and you may have never discovered it. When you honestly don't know where you are most gifted, you are free to experiment with some things to find out the things at which you're really good.

Caution: Some people spend their entire lives searching for this to no avail. Discovering your gifts should be a prayerful and intentional process.

Remember that you have a short time on campus to impact people for God's glory. So time is of the essence! Also, your giftings are to be used for God! That is the essential part. You are gifted for His purpose because He wants you to use them for His glory. Yes, you can be gifted in an area that is not directly spiritual. In our golf example, the playing of golf may not draw people to Christ, but the conversations and relationships built on the course could have an eternal impact. There should be no pride in this discovery, but it should be met with praise and thanksgiving to God for what He has given you whether He did it supernaturally or through the process of genetics. To not accept His talents is sin (Matt. 25:14-30). We make what He has placed in our hands something small and meaningless when we are prideful. It's like saying, "I don't need God because I did that all by myself." The same is true when we don't embrace and acknowledge the talents He has placed in us. So, whether you know your strengths or are not sure, you have your work cut out for you. What better joy does a person get than when they have given someone a gift and see them fully using it for its purposes? "God has given us different gifts for doing certain things well." Romans 12:6 (NLT)

One very good place to begin looking for talents is with your parents. Did you grow up in a family who communicated very well? Is everyone very articulate and well-read? This may be a way to develop you into very good communicator. Home is a fine place to discover your exceptionality. Do you come from a family of couch potatoes who watch a whole lot of television? This was my family. This could lead you in the direction of television production. Some people would discount an upbringing like mine, but that may be an area you need to investigate. Face it. For good or bad, your parents are your parents, and they were used by God to implant a specific unique DNA code in you. You are your father's and mother's child, whether or not you even know them.

The second obvious place to look for these abilities would be God Himself. There are things He places in you at salvation that He wants you to use for His plans for your life and your campus. He is the designer of your destiny, and you have within you what you need to accomplish His goals for you on campus and in life. Start with the manufacturer. The question is, "What am I supposed to do?" It starts from within. Don't get lost in the hustle and movement on campus and waste your time. You are supposed to reach the lost and love God with all you have. Start there for motivation and look at your giftedness for your unique talents to accomplish these goals. Your campus will be changed through your style, flare, and creativity. The sky is the limit when you work within your own skills.

Passion

What stirs your heart? _____

_____

What gets you excited? _____

_____

What makes you mad? _____

_____

What makes you cry? _____

_____

That is probably your area of passion. God uses these things to keep us motivated and focused when establishing God-inspired impact. Your passion is where you are drawn naturally and that thing you think about most of the time. We sometimes waste passion in pursuits that don't account for much eternally. If we can realign them for God's purpose, the possibilities are limitless (as in my TV scenario).

Your ability to find your passion area has major implications for your life and for your campus effectiveness. We have all heard of the mid-life crisis. This happens to those roughly between the ages of 40 and 55. It happens when people realize they are half way through their lives and they are less than satisfied with what they have done and are doing. They are left to try and align their lives with the things they are most passionate about. This is often dramatic and abrupt. They are feverishly searching for what will make them both happy and give them a sense of purpose and significance.

This is happening at a smaller scale much sooner for twenty-somethings. It's called a quarter-life crisis. Many young adults after college are beginning to wonder what their lives will be. They may have a degree in an area that they aren't passionate about, or they may not able to find a job in their field of study. These twenty-somethings are usually tired of the "party scene." They have done it. There is a growing discontent for meaning-less sexual encounters, and there is an increasing desire to settle down and truly grow up. They are looking to make their lives count for more than what they are experiencing. This is the quarter-life crisis.

You can avoid this crisis by first pouring your life into Jesus now and then into your passion areas. It's been said that when you find what you love you will never work another day in your life. Retirement isn't even a thought when you live from a place of passion! Think about it, why would someone want to leave a "job" when they love what they do? So what is it? What is the one thing that you would love to do for the rest of your life? If money were not an issue, what would you do for free? Even if you love to make money that is fine, but the principle still applies. Making and wanting to make money is not in any way evil or inherently bad. It's when you begin to love money that is the root of all kinds of evil.

> "For the love of money is the root of all kinds of evil. Some people, eager for money, have wandered from the faith and pierced themselves with many griefs."
>
> 1 Timothy 6:10 (NIV)

The challenge is that we sometimes only see ministry or God's work as the one thing that should be desired as a passion. This is the wrong way to approach things. If you love children, you don't need to work at a church day care to honor God. Maybe you should open your own daycare or be a school teacher or a great parent! The choices are as varied as your imagination. This is just in the area of children. Please understand that this is not a slap at the church. I love the church and find great joy in serving in my local congregation. But, when we think we can only serve God within the confines of a church service, we limit our own effectiveness and our overall kingdom impact. Not only that, we can miss opportunities to impact the world. It's hopefully a wake-up call and an encouragement to you. Think about it…if all the believers worked solely at the church, who would be left to engage with the culture on a day to day basis? You can start exercising this right now on your campus and be used to make a difference. It's simple. "Commit your actions to the LORD, and your plans will succeed." Proverbs 16:3 (NLT)

You have some passion that is God-honoring. Whether or not you see it as spiritual is all in your perspective. Someone wants to be a choreographer, someone else a chef, and another a graphic designer. God can get glory from it all. Now, if your passion is to be an accountant, it would not be God-honoring to cheat and steal from people. But if you love to make sure that the debits and credits are correct, that's God-honoring. You can make a name for yourself as an honest accountant who loves God.

Caution: Never allow your passion to outweigh your desire to please God. The first of the Ten Commandments is, "You shall have no other gods before me."

God is and always should be first. Once you have that right, the sky is the limit. God wants you to pour your energies into some work. It may be ministry as a vocation, but if it's not then that's fine also. The point is to find something you love to do and do it! The college campus is the perfect opportunity to allow God to use your gifts to magnify Himself. He can and will use your abilities to reach your campus.

Experiences

While you're doing a personal heart check, look at your experiences, both the good and bad. This may seem basic, but more than often our experiences lead us to our destiny. It can certainly lead you to campus impact. Search your past for markers and signs to help you find your talents. Were you in the audio/visual club in high school? Have you ever gotten in trouble for trying to take your radio apart? You may have a passion for electronics. Have you always had animals and when you see images of animals in distress your heart breaks? This could reveal your leaning toward veterinary medicine or animal rehab and rescue. Our past has a lot to do with our future. If you haven't chosen one already, this search can lead you toward a major.

Inevitably when thinking about your experiences, your mind goes to negative ones. That is fine, also. **God does not waste one experience!** Your pain can produce passion in your life. You may not have had a father in your home, but God can use that to direct you toward helping men engage in the lives their own children. There may be abuse in your past. That can be used to build a heart of advocacy for those in similar situations. This is where many people check out mentally because the pain of the past can at times seem too great. Please don't run from this process which can be very painful, no matter how difficult. Overcoming these types of challenges is necessary for your health and development. Get counseling if you need to but face it to defeat it!

The Bible is not absent of instruction when it comes to issues of our past. One of the best examples of this type of resiliency in scripture is Joseph. Take some time to read the whole story starting in Genesis chapters 37 through 50. Basically, Joseph was his father's favorite, and this didn't sit well with his older brothers. To add insult to injury, Joseph was given dreams by God that showed how he would become greater than his brothers. In response, he was sold into slavery by his brother. Then, he was accused of trying to sleep with his boss's wife, and neglected in prison. He eventually became the second most important man in Egypt and his brothers came to him asking for assistance. Instead of repaying the evil that was done to him, look at his response.

> "You intended to harm me, but God intended
> it for good to accomplish what is not being
> done, the saving of many lives."
> Genesis 50:20 (Message)

God turned everything around for him. Not only was his family saved from a killer drought, but all of Egypt was saved, too! Can God use your painful experiences to save someone else?

Once again, this may be a very hard process to go through, so get help if you need to. There is no shame in asking for the help. It's more important to be the person God wants you to be so you can advance his kingdom on your campus and in the world. Speak to a mentor, church leader, or a Christian counselor if you need to, but don't withhold help and healing from those who are supposed to learn and grow through your experiences.

It is important for you to invest time in investigating your experiences because your past is a part of your story. It does not have to define you! But it is a part of you, ultimately for your good. Not to mention, others need to hear your story. In the end, your story matters to others. People will learn from your successes and failures and if they are wise will apply those principles to their lives. **Remember, average people learn from their own mistakes, smart people learn from the mistakes of others.** "And they overcame by the blood of the Lamb and by the word of their testimony" Revelation 12:11 (KJV).

Someone on your campus may be hurting, and they need your words of encouragement. There is probably someone who is considering suicide, and to hear what you have dealt with that in your life may give them hope. There is undoubtedly someone on your campus that was abused, hurt, and scared by life. The key to their freedom in Christ may be your story of victory in spite of your circumstances. Your pain is powerful. Even if you are not over the sting, someone may need to hear that God cares enough to walk them through it. Your experiences count and matter to God. You would be surprised to know how many people just need to know that they are not struggling alone. Some feel abandoned by God, and they may only see His care and receive His comfort if they see His light in your eyes.

I grew up without a father. I was born out of an adulterous relationship and because of that my father abandoned me. Without that support, I grew up in low income housing and on welfare. I know what it's like to be both homeless and hungry. At times I still see the impact of my fatherless childhood in my life, but now my story gives hope to others. I have an opportunity to take that bad situation in my life and allow God to shine in spite of it. Even people who don't have that type of experience can find comfort in the fact that we are not alone no matter the difficulty of the background. This is how God can take the mess of our past and create a masterpiece for His glory. People around you need to hear that it's a message of hope!

If this is not your experience and you have not yet had any times that cause great pain, then rejoice and be ready if and when it comes. It's a fact of life that hard times come for us all. God can still use you to display His keeping power. No matter where you are on the spectrum of human experience, everything you have gone through can be used to display the wonder of God and serve as a guide to your passion.

Abilities

This portion of your passion hunt is not complicated at all. The basic question is, "What can you do?" Do you know how to fix a car or care for flowers? Your abilities should be based on things in which you have shown a level of proficiency. Unlocking your passion may be sitting right in front of you. There is nothing more frustrating as a college pastor than to see a student change their major five times because they don't have a clue what they want to do with their lives. I tend to always take them through what they know they can and enjoy doing. It's that simple.

Please be careful not to make the same mistake in reverse. For instance, you probably know people who think they can sing. They grew up singing in church. Everyone in their family told them they can sing, but the sad truth is they can't at all. When you hear them sing, you want to tear your own ears off in an attempt to stop the pain of it all. Some people are simply blind to the fact that they are not good at some things. It's sad but true. There should be people that love you enough to tell you the truth to confirm your "abilities." You should have people in your life who will not allow you to "believe your own press." Do you have anyone in your life who will tell you the truth even when it hurts? These are perfect candidates to help you confirm you abilities. There are not many things scarier than someone who has an over inflated since of talent.

Caution: You may have a skill and it may not be developed as of yet. Just because you don't see the fruit of your ability that does not mean you don't have it.

Getting good, honest feedback comes in handy. Some people give up before they try. Take a chance to see what lives within. This makes life fun and increases your experiences. Don't forget that we are in a search for your heart's passion so that you can more effectively reach your campus. Some things you find out only by taking chances. This is a benefit to college. A chance in college is called an elective. No one will think any less of you for taking a chance called pottery or photography or Russian. Have at it. You may not discover your life's passion, but you may get a good glimpse of that in which you stink. You may get an idea that will give you a ministry in which you can serve while at school. You won't know unless you try. TAKE A CHANCE!

Style

Your personal style is just that, your personal style. When looking at your campus and the needs that should be met, it's always good to look into your style or way of doing things. God will often use the style you have to express Himself through you. The difficulty for most college students is that they are still developing a sense of style. That's fine and normal, but you want to take time to discover your own way of doing things.

When people think of style they usually think of one thing: clothing. Well, that's not necessarily what I mean by style although it does apply. It's more your "way," or your preferred leanings. It's the expression of your personality in the things you do. For example, let's say that you are going to gather people for the purpose of prayer. Some people will decide to connect with the campus ministries and come to the center of the campus and pray. Another may gather a group of three or four people and go to the highest place on campus and pray at night. Still others may coordinate a scheduled early morning prayer and have people rising up early in their own rooms all around campus and pray at the same time. With passion to pray, those were three completely different expressions of style. You should look at your personality, experiences, passion, and preferences to find your style. They all work together and can be used to help you find your voice on campus. Some are loud and others subdued, but the point is to express you. God wants to use you, authentically you, to make some impact on your campus. He is not getting rid of who you are; He will use who you are.

Caution: This does not mean that there won't be times when you feel led to do something that is the opposite of what you would naturally do.

God sent Peter to reach out to Jews when his personality and demeanor would have led him toward the Gentiles. He took Paul, who was well versed in Jewish laws and ways to the Gentiles. So don't use your style as an excuse to keep you from reaching those to whom God is calling you. If you feel that God is calling you to reach out to football players, then do it. It does not matter if you don't even know what a football looks like. He can use the most unlikely people to do the most amazing things.

This should serve as an encouragement to be you. God made you the way He made you for a reason. Your campus needs to see Christ in you! Yes, they need to see Christ first, but they see Him expressed through you. Never discount the part you play in the story of God.

You must discover your heart's passion. You are gifted by God. He will use your gifts to stir passion within you. He is wise enough to use both your positive and negative experiences. God will allow you to develop your abilities and style to shine as bright as you can for Him. Always live from your heart for Him. Your campus needs it!

Life's Passion

Please understand that finding your life's passion will take you far beyond your college career. If you can discover and live out of your heart's passions while a student, it prepares you for your life's purpose. If you can find interests and concerns that grab your attention that is a large part of fulfilling God's personal plan for your entire life. The average Christian has an inkling of what contribution they want to make to society. But, you have the opportunity to develop your skills in that area to ensure greater success.

Everything you are learning now is meant to be used in your career, family, church and the world. If you take full advantage of what has been given to you, you will be well on you way to having a fulfilling life. God loves you and He wants not only your college years but all your years to matter. It's His amazing grace that allows you to embrace what He has for you at such an early age so that you can make the most of what God has given you.

I love what the Bible says about David.

> "For David, after he had served God's will and purpose and counsel in his own generation, fell asleep [in death] and was buried among his forefathers..."
>
> Acts 13:36 (Amplified)

As flawed as David was as a human being, he was able to fulfill his purpose in the earth. I want that to be said of me when I die. You should want that said about you. The great

news is that while you're in college, you can explore your areas
of interest, so you can find your heart's passions, more easily
than most. God made you the way He did on purpose and
He wants you to utilize everything He has placed in you. Your
passions matter to God.

CLASS ACT

There has been a ton of grade improvement products developed over the past few years. They will cost you a nominal fee of $19.95 or 12 easy installments of $29.99. Did you know that you can purchase memorization CDs that will allow you to retain everything you read from now until eternity? It will even work in heaven! Call now, supplies are low... We have all heard the marketing pitches for these programs. The bottom line is there are products that will allow you to bring up your grade point average.

I'm not necessarily knocking learning tools. There just might be a better way. That way is called... your parents! "If you don't get on the dean's list then I am taking your car away." Now that's motivation. Better yet, how about getting a letter from your school saying you have lost your scholarship or, worse, are being removed from the school roster due to academic ineligibility. Is that motivation? But here's number one: The greatest motivator possible, God, is looking at your school work and wants you to represent Him well. How does that sit with you? That should be the greatest motivator ever. All mighty God is watching your grades because they reflect Him because you reflect Him.

This is strange to some. You may ask 'How do my academics apply to my love for God and my witness to unbelievers?' In this chapter we will see how your academics are important to God. We know how our fasting and praying reflect God, but how can something as non-spiritual as academics impact my faith and that of others? To answer that question we must break apart the concept. We must look at how it both reflects worship and impacts your witness to the world.

To embrace the full effect of how class work and worship are connected, we must go to the scriptures. When David was dying and prepared to bless his son, Solomon, he shared this to him.

> "So be strong, show yourself a man, and observe what the Lord your God requires: walk in His ways and keep His decrees and commands, His laws and His requirements as written in the Law of Moses, so that you may prosper in all you do and wherever you go...
>
> 1 Kings 2:2–3; NIV

The spiritual advice David gave Solomon was to show yourself a man (basically grow up). Obey God, and walk with God.

It was all for the purpose that Solomon would prosper everywhere he went. I don't know about you, but I want to prosper everywhere I go! The charge David gives to grow up and follow God's commands is the type of thing we love to embrace. But the fruit of that is shown when we actually start to prosper wherever we go. We are to excel in our grades because it shows that we are committed to Christ in every area of our lives. There are, of course, always "extenuating circumstances," but let's just look at the scripture for what it says and see ourselves in the light of it.

We can easily see the correlation between our work and worship when it relates to our careers. God is who we are really working for. A college student's job is their school work. Yes, you may have a job at a local coffee shop, but your primary goal and focus is school. Your professors are in essence your supervisors. It's a job. There is money being exchanged for goods and services provided. You are submitted to that professor for as long as you have that class. If you indeed ultimately work for the Lord, what grade does God give you for your service to Him in the classroom? How does He see your grades? This is not always fun to consider, but it's God to whom we must answer.

All Eyes on Me

There is another reason Christians should excel academically. It's because others are looking at our examples and will determine if they should listen to our Gospel message based on what they see in us. Some will try to rationalize away the call to exceed academically, but we can't run from the fact that we

are the living epistles that people look to for spiritual guidance.
You can not have a "Do as I say and not as I do" mentality.
That never really flies. Let's look at what the word of God says
on the matter.

> "Live an exemplary life among the nations so
> that your actions will refute their prejudice.
> Then they'll be won over to God's side and be
> there to join the celebration when He arrives."
>
> I Peter 2:12, (Message)

Our actions speak louder than words. Yes, we need to communicate the Good News of the Son of God. But our lives
must be in sync with that same message, and our grades are
one action that shouts loud. Just to be clear, people can and
do come to faith through the efforts of flunking Christians. It
happens all the time. There are simply less barriers when the
believer has a report of all A's. For some reading this, there is
a resounding, "YES!" Others are filled with "buts" and "what
abouts," but that's alright. Think about it this way, what do we
say to the professor who is giving us the sub-par grades? What
do they think about the God that we say we serve? Have you
earned an audience with your professors based on the grades
they give you? It's just a thought.

**There are many intellectuals in our society that think
that Christianity is a faith for morons.** Smart people are at
best agnostics in these people's minds. This is in no way true,
but those who are in place to communicate the truth of the

scriptures can be easily written off because of their lack of academic studiousness.

To the intellectual unbeliever, a Christian can read nothing but the Bible. This should break our hearts because who is going to reach them if not us? It affects others when you are in class and you don't submit your work. Your class work may mean more than you know. Are you open to doing better if it will mean that it might increase your sphere of influence? Later in this chapter, you will get some tips as to how to maximize your academic pursuits.

It's All Relative

Eventually, two objections come up concerning academics. The first is, "I am in engineering school," or "I'm in Ivy League school," so it's just harder. The second is like it, "I'm taking physics or anthropology, and it's too hard to expect A's in those classes." That sounds so good! But both are cop-outs. Now the math majors are all ready to burn this book! Seriously, the Bible helps us with this, too. Here's the principle: you do what you are equipped to do. English majors are not inferior to engineering majors in intelligence. Nor is a Pre-Med major any smarter necessarily than a Communications major. We all have different talents and gifts from God. One person will struggle with writing 25 papers in one week, and another will lose it over compound mathematical equations. This does not mean that we all have the same intelligence level. Just that we get what we get to do what we have to do. Let's learn from the parable of the talents found in Matthew 25:14–28 (NIV).

"Again, it (The Kingdom of God) will be like a man going on a journey, who called his servants and entrusted his property to them. To one he gave five talents of money, to another two talents, and to another one talent, each according to his ability. Then he went on his journey. The man who had received the five talents went at once and put his money to work and gained five more. So also, the one with the two talents gained two more. But the man who had received the one talent went off, dug a hole in the ground and hid his master's money.

"After a long time the master of those servants returned and settled accounts with them. The man who had received the five talents brought the other five. 'Master,' he said, 'you entrusted me with five talents. See, I have gained five more.'

"His master replied, 'Well done, good and faithful servant! You have been faithful with a few things; I will put you in charge of many things. Come and share your master's happiness!' "The man with the two talents also came. 'Master,' he said, 'you entrusted me with two talents; see, I have gained two more.' "His master replied, 'Well done, good and faithful servant! You have been faithful with a few

things; I will put you in charge of many things.
Come and share your master's happiness!'

"Then the man who had received the one talent
came. 'Master,' he said, 'I knew that you are a
hard man, harvesting where you have not sown
and gathering where you have not scattered
seed. So I was afraid and went out and hid your
talent in the ground. See, here is what belongs
to you.' His master replied, 'You wicked, lazy
servant! So you knew that I harvest where I have
not sown and gather where I have not scattered
seed? Well then, you should have put my money on deposit with the bankers, so that when
I returned I would have received it back with
interest. Take the talent from him and give it to
the one who has the ten talents. For everyone
who has will be given more, and he will have an
abundance. Whoever does not have, even what
he has will be taken from him.'"

No one can determine how much they get from God.
All we can do is work with what He gives us so that we can
increase it for His purposes. Our society places a high priority
on majors, not God. If He wants you to discover the cure for
cancer or write a screenplay that magnifies Him, then fulfill
that purpose. The man that was given two pieces of money was
judged based on the amount given. It's all relative. If someone
is just outrageously gifted by God and they get straight A's

but is gifted enough to get straight A's, that is where God's standard is for them. Even if your school does not recognize (+) and (-)'s, the point is God must be pleased! Is what we give Him a good offering and is what you do showing people the God we say we love?

We should no longer look to others and say we are doing well based on their progress or the lack thereof. We as humans always only look at the outside, but God looks at the heart. Please don't lose the point. We are looking to impact the campus for God's sake. It will take us thinking about things differently than everyone else sees things. It's pride that would make us think that since we have different capabilities and callings and majors that we should get special attention or respect.

You should embrace your lot and give God your best in your grades or whatever you are learning for that matter. So, no longer look at others and say, "Well, you're an art major so that's why you are doing well." When you are tempted to say that, just try and imagine yourself painting the Mona Lisa or sculpting a work of art like the famous David. Do you see? It's all relative to what God has placed in you.

There is a young lady that I know, and we will call her Dina. She was a straight A student. Her grades were made known to a group of other students in a conference setting, and they were just floored at her academic success. Upon further examination, it was discovered that she was given more time to complete her class work than other students. Then everyone with one sigh went "oh well, that's why". What I haven't told you is that she was legally blind. She was given more time because it took her more time to read her materials than it took the rest of us. She did not ask to be patted on the back or celebrated; she simply did the work placed before her. Some would focus on the fact that she is blind, and it's amazing that she could go to class and compete with seeing colleagues and out-do them. Others would look at the additional time she has been given and say, "Well, that's not fair and you should not place her efforts next to her classmates." She would simply get her work done to the best of her ability because God was watching. While others wasted time, she studied. Dina was active in her campus ministry and had great grades. The same God that allowed her to be blind was expecting her to honor Him and be a witness to others. You truly receive the abilities you have from God, and to Him the fruit of those abilities will be presented. So, work for God's approval because He is the one who it should be for in the first place.

Reclaiming Academic Excellence

So what can be done for the person who is having a difficult time honoring God academically? One thing is to find out what helps you learn best. A big problem with many of the different study guides is that we all have different styles of learning. Not everyone gains knowledge or maintains it the same way. If you are an audio/visual learner, a lot of book work may be kryptonite to your academic career. You may need to select an instructor that teaches in a class setting very well. That will give you more of an opportunity to excel scholastically.

You must not only know how you are wired, but you should also do your research on ways you can succeed in unfavorable learning environments. Let's look at this further. A bookworm who loves the written word may find nothing but frustration from a professor who is bent on teaching things that are not in the text. These people will pour over a book and come to the test only to find themselves at a loss. This is not from failure to study. It's a failure of matching of teaching style and learning style. It may be to your benefit to research your individual learning style.

This is often an issue when you've chosen the wrong school. There are some large schools that don't lean toward classroom instruction. They're more of the sort to not count class attendance; it's simply not important in the school's environment. Smaller schools, due to their environment, can focus more on face-to-face interaction. Now, this is not a rule because there are large schools that pride themselves on individual attention and small ones that have a reputation for primarily independent work. The message is that you must find what will help you the most in whatever environment in which you find yourself.

What is the recourse for the person who believes that they are at the right school and are in the right situation and still can't gain any ground scholastically? There is a still hope and a way to win. It's simple. Find a way! You may be thinking, "Now that doesn't help." Diligence is the key here. There are ways to find people who are amazing in whatever field of study in which you are finding difficulty. Find someone who will be able to help you. This takes humility and a hunger to overcome your academic deficiency.

Go to your department's office and ask for a tutor. Most schools have tutorial programs; you need only to sign up to get help. There are no excuses for not getting the help needed. If someone in your class is doing exceptionally well, ask for their help. Believer or unbeliever, you might be gaining some ground into a new sphere of influence. Sometimes God uses our vulnerability and submission to preach for us. It's about Him being magnified, remember. He can use your current subpar grades and your determination to overcome to speak volumes for Him.

Another suggestion is to go to your professor and ask for help. Once again, in a large school, a large class, or with an unavailable teacher, this may be difficult. Diligence is most important in this type of situation. Usually, you can at least connect with a teaching assistant (a graduate student assigned to help an instructor) for the class.

Here is a thought. At the beginning of the semester/quarter, ask an important question of the professor: "What should I do in your class to achieve?" This is one of the best questions that can be asked. Sometimes a professor will say, "Study harder," or "Study smarter," which doesn't really help you. More often than not, you will get some great advice for a favorable outcome. Even if this does not work, it will often make you more memorable to that teacher which could give you a little grace if or when needed.

Consider sitting in the front of the class. When the presentation is not the most exciting, this can keep you from daydreaming or getting distracted. In middle school, the cool kids may have sat in the back of the class, but in higher education, that is often reversed. The good students sit in the front. Don't just sit passively in front either. Sit on the edge of your seat like a tiger about to pounce. This posture can enhance your readiness to receive information. To add to that, ask questions even when you think you know the answer to what you are asking. In higher education, some instructors don't allow questions. If they do, great, jump in. If you get the answer wrong, find out why. Crucify your embarrassment for the sake of excellence. When questions are not asked, you ask a question. This may once again make your face and your tenacity memorable for a professor who may lose your face in the crowd of others.

Please be encouraged if you have a heart to succeed academically, but your grades don't reflect it. This portion of the book is not meant to induce guilt, but to cause action. I struggled though many of these issues as a student. I was an average student in high school and had to beg to get into college. What I did was understand my learning style, and used that to my advantage. I received help from students, professors, graduate assistants, and church members. I was so intent on honoring God with my grades that many people assumed that I was a straight "A" student even though at times I was fighting to get a "B." So I know you can do this!

I came into my academic rhythm in college. I didn't come from a home where education was valued. But, in college I worked harder than most students. It took me so long to get my academic act together that by my third year I needed to take six classes plus labs and projects to graduate close to the scheduled time. I knew that God would be prouder of my hard working "B" than he would a lazy one. I just wanted to please

God and not embarrass Him by marring my testimony through my grades. If I can do it, there truly is hope for anyone.

Top of the Class

On the other hand, for those who are excelling scholastically, this is your time to shine and not gloat or look down on others. This is a moment to advance the kingdom. Yes, through academic excellence, but so much more. For example, you are now in a place to offer your services as either an official or unofficial tutor. There are, and always will be, students who have a difficult time making the grade. How Godly is it to serve others who need your help? That's the Kingdom in motion. Jesus came to save others who were unable to save themselves. You have just set yourself up to be a minister of class work. Don't squander the opportunity. This can be a challenge for many because we are hard-wired to think about ourselves and no one else. That is anti-Christ. What if Jesus would have done that? Okay, okay, this is not a spanking; it's an encouragement to use the gift God has given you to serve others. It's an hour a week that could change someone's entire destiny.

Here are a few ways to leverage your grades:

Hold a study group. Get a group of people together for the purpose of work. You can wear your Christian t-shirt or lead the group in prayer before you study. People are usually very open to prayer when they are struggling academically. If you choose to pray, please don't pray an hour-long prayer. This is not your moment to pray that they would stop being such a filthy, dirty sinner. It's a moment to sow a seed of a love and dependence toward God. It needs to be less than a minute long and God-focused.

You may want to consider being a tutor for other students in your classes and/or develop a group of tutors that serve both the college and the surrounding middle and high schools. Now that's impact! Create a test library. Most schools have no problem with people keeping old tests and sharing them.

Caution: This is not a license to cheat. If your school has a policy against test libraries, then please disregard this suggestion.

Many textbooks change from year to year and information changes slightly, but old tests are good study guides. If as an upper classman, you make your old tests available to younger students; you have made yourself a resource for those coming behind you. If you are in an organization, then you can get your colleagues to compile tests from different disciplines and now you are the pillar of educational success.

In addition to that, there may be another opportunity for kingdom advancement. That is instructor outreach. This usually happens at non-Christian schools, where a great portion of professors are not believers. Some even use the classroom to preach their anti-God rhetoric (we will address that in a moment). Exceptional students can sometimes be held as a favorite of a teacher. Some will call you a teacher's pet or brown-noser, but this is a position of great honor and influence. Rarely, if ever, do professors use the classroom as an opportunity to learn. They usually see it as, "I have the information, and you must listen to what I say." A student who has earned his/her teacher's respect can be used to share truth and light. Not every teacher/pupil relationship ends there, but the opportunity is available more than you might think. It's a possible window to share your passion for God and compassion toward them.

Why is this important? Some anti-God teachers will use their platform of a school environment to spew their philosophies. Others will sadly go home to an empty existence without any expressions of true love. Still, some will not just inject their lectures with unspiritual rhetoric, but they will influence others whose spiritual foundation may not be strong. Professors need Jesus, too. They are a part of your mission field.

You can not fall prey to the Almighty Teacher Syndrome. Many people are no longer walking with God because of what someone who "supposedly" knew more than them said. There is nothing sadder. Do you realize that you can respectfully challenge your professors? This is not an endorsement to be obnoxious or overly dogmatic in any way. We should always walk in meekness, which is teach-ability. That doesn't mean that you should allow someone to disrespect your spiritual beliefs either. This can be more of an issue on secular campuses, although not all Christian campuses function from a Biblical framework in the classroom.

This is not high school! You are expected to have some level of challenge in the collegiate environment. One of my lost teachers was a religion professor. He had abandoned the call of God on His life, and he was teaching us from his agnostic point of view. I so enjoyed asking him questions and standing up to him because I am, in part, a trouble maker. But, greater

than that, other students were looking to him to be the Bible
scholar, and he had only minimal knowledge of the true and
living God. By the end of that class, I not only stood out in the
minds of the other students, but I had gained the respect and
admiration of that professor.

Your biggest challenge may be, not knowing what you
believe. It may not be the fact that the instructor has more
knowledge than you; it's that they know what they believe
more than you know what you believe. That's why Paul's letter
to Timothy should encourage you.

> "Study to shew thyself approved unto God,
> a workman that needeth not to be ashamed,
> rightly dividing the word of truth."
> 2 Timothy 2:15 (KJV)

Have you studied the word of God? Whether or not you are
an A or D- student, do you know what you believe? Do you
have any doubt concerning the virgin birth, the substitution-
ary atonement of Jesus, the resurrection of Christ? If you are
not solid on the basics of scripture, whether you know it or not,
you are already defeated.

It's very good and God-honoring to get exceptional grades.
It should not supersede Biblical knowledge. We as Christians
can't throw our brains away when it comes to spiritual matters.
Only when we have a Biblical worldview can we make a difference in the class for Jesus. Then you can more clearly see when
someone is covertly or overtly defaming the name of Christ
and have an answer for all challengers. Not that you must have

an answer to everything, but rather you should at least know the basics. It's critically important that you know the basis of your faith. Be a scholar when it comes to your class work and be a student of the word of God. Honor God with your intellect. It will open doors of ministry that will amaze you.

PECULIAR
POLITICS

When thinking about the landscape of influence on campuses around the country, one major area is student government. Not everyone who serves in public leadership is cut out for the political arena. However if you are a good fit, there are some serious opportunities for visible significant kingdom advancement. Hopefully, over the course of this chapter you might feel the tug toward elected leadership on your campus. Maybe you will better understand the breadth of visibility and responsibility which is resident through your student government. It's an opportunity to serve your campus, the entire campus, in a big way.

Let's start at the place of service. Many people who are interested in politics nationally get jaded and cynical at the corruption that takes place in the political system. The challenge is, sometimes it happens on a micro level in the collegiate system as well. I don't say that to produce cynicism in you; it's simply the truth. That is why you may be needed. The issue is one of service. Those in political positions are supposed to be public servants. Instead, some only serve themselves. This is an area where you may be able to infuse honesty and integrity. As it pertains to influence, one of the most direct ways you can make a difference is as an elected official. **Politicians are upfront and in the lime light. Handled appropriately, they can shine a great light on Christ.**

Jesus himself sets the record straight about service and visibility. "But he that is greatest among you shall be your servant." Matthew 23:11 (KJV) There is greatness for the sake of Christ that is available; it starts by serving in the name of Jesus. It's sad that people use service to try to make themselves great, when God often magnifies and illuminates people's service. Everything they need is in Him. If you heed the call to service through your student government association, there is much to gain.

There is a need for committed, submitted, and helps-based leadership on your campus. This is not an assumption that your campus-elected officials are corrupt. A better way to think about it is this: someone will decide where the resources for your campus activities will go. If it is being squandered, then that stops when you get in office (or it should). The more important issue is that you can guide the activities for your campus. Think about it. Really consider the fact that someone will guide the ship. There will be a person who will say, "Yeah, I'll be the president." Someone else will say, "Sure, *why not?*" I can in some way choose where the activities funds will go, *ok.* Others still will love the fact that everyone else will know and follow them. Who will see this opportunity, for the sake of Jesus, to speak to the body, and lead the student closer to him? We need Christians in leadership in the political realm.

Say Something

Before we all go charging into the student activities center to sign up for the next election, you might want to know a few things. There is nothing worse than a well meaning believer who with a "charge from God" (I use that loosely) jumps into the public arena with nothing to say except Jesus loves you. This is not to place any negative correlations on that statement. It's just that if you are not up to date on issues, needs, and concerns of the student body, then you have nothing to say.

Some really radical believers try to run for office just to have a voice to say great Biblical statements like that. That may hurt the Kingdom cause more than help it. In rare situations, this approach may have some traction; however, how much more influence could you have if you say Jesus loves you and here is a plan for campus advancement. It's a question of quality.

People run after great moments for impact, but our cause for Christian leadership leans more toward sustained influence. Short-term impact has its place, but the long-term commitment shows character and quality that the world is looking for in Christ. This means that we will need to actually use our brains and research and develop skills to answer hard questions. Let's think about it another way. What if a person was running for mayor of your city and their only reason for joining the campaign was Jesus loves you? Great, Jesus loves me but what about education? What about the 102 abandoned buildings in our fair town? The point is that we want them to be prepared to earn our vote. As a Christian, do you want to vote for another Christian who has nothing to say? In these positions, you have the mandate to say something of quality.

How can you make sure you have done your due diligence in preparation? One way to increase your effectiveness is to find out the critical needs of the campus. Is there a large drop out level in first-year students? If so, what can be done about that? Why is this happening? Who is it affecting? To what stimuli does that segment of the school population respond and how can you get support to them? A leader has to look at all sides of these types of concerns. This also works if you are not running for student government. This is a skill critical for strategic outreach, period. As a political figure, you must explain your strategies to those from whom you are soliciting a vote.

Political Insider

My friend Dover was a great example of what a Christian should be on a college campus. He was known as a bit of an agitator on campus. There was a terrible student government president in the office on our campus. Dover decided that he would do something about it. So he jumped into the race. The problem was, other than being prepared to speak on moral issues surrounding the current administration, he had little

more to say. Not that he was not smart enough to really deal
with the other issues surrounding the campus population. He
just was not ready for that level of engagement.

He was greatly respected by all. So, people did not openly
say that they wanted him to talk about all the concerns they
had. Dover was just happy to be able to vocalize the problems
and bring them to light. But, he could have changed the school
at large and led them into a brighter future. If he would have
been better equipped, he may have won. That's the difference.

My wife Zarat, on the other hand, took her campus by force.
She, as a freshman, volunteered to serve the student government leadership. She became well versed in all the major issues
concerning the students. She got a pulse on the needs and
wants of that collegiate community. In her fourth year, she was
president and was able to creatively use her influence on campus to shine her light for Jesus. She was able to bring Christian
business leaders to the campus to speak, allocate funds for a
spiritual event during homecoming, and was a personal mentor
for many students. That is influence. She even had an audience
with the Board of Trustees and the President of the school.

Can somebody say "influence!" It's years later, and she still
gets stopped by people who remember her and were touched
by her impact.

The two are studies in contrast. They were both strong
Christians and looked up to by many. They were both clear on
the fact that God wanted to use His people to leverage them for
His sake. But, Zarat was prepared for the rigor of an election
and the office of student body president.

Leading Up & Down

What many don't realize is the massive trust and responsibility given to student government associations. You will be in the presence of many leaders from several industries and CEOs of fortune 500 companies that serve on Trustee Boards for colleges and universities. As a representative of your school, you have a chance to touch the lives of people who set policy for countries. That's global impact. You could be used by God to say something that could alter a CEO's point of view. This is not over reaching. It's how things get done at numbers of schools. There is a saying, "It's not what you know. It's who you know." By embracing the call for political leadership on your campus, you could come to know great people, and with that comes great influence.

When you compound that with the audience you get with the administrators and president and the opportunity to really affect change for next generations of students to come, why wouldn't you try it? Most administrators use student government to get a pulse on the collegiate body. They are more prone to take suggestions from students involved politically than they are an average Joe Christian student. You could be a voice for the Christian organizations that are overlooked and neglected populations on your campus. Student government leaders are in the perfect place to offer those suggestions.

You also can set yourself up as the liaison for incoming students. The elected student leaders are usually the face of the institution. They will sometimes be awarded the opportunity to speak at campus-wide events. When first-year students arrive, they are usually looking for mentors, and student government officers are some of the most visible positions.

There will be a Student Government president next year, an entire cabinet, and, depending on the school, maybe even a board of advisors. You will be subject to someone's leadership for good or bad next session. Look at what the Bible says about governing leadership.

> "Let every person be subject to the governing authorities. For there is no authority except from God, and those that exist have been instituted by God."
>
> Romans 13:1 (ESV)

The question is could that, or should that, be you. Not everyone is able to hold such positions, and if you're not one of them, then that is perfectly fine. I wasn't. But, if you are, then get started. God has need of you.

HOMECOMING

We as humans enjoy a place where we can rest and be at home. It's there that we often have our defenses down, and home is the perfect place to reach people for Christ. Many campuses have residence halls where a great number of the students spend the bulk of their time. Home is the place where people usually completely open their hearts. If you can find a way to leverage your influence in campus housing, you may see great opportunity for impact in people's lives. If you are not on campus, then there are still some other ways in which you can have effect also.

Residence halls are where a lot of quality relationships are developed and where much of the opinions and view points are really discussed. Make no mistake about it. The classroom starts conversations that can radically alter people's worldviews for good or bad. But, those conversations are often carried into the living quarters and expanded upon and processed further. It's a great place to direct ideologies toward the one that will matter most.

In order to capitalize on these opportunities, you have to start talking to people. **You may have an introverted personality, but that should not be a barrier from you telling people about the God who loves them and sacrificed His son for their eternal hope and total bliss with Him.** You will be amazed at how people will speak to you just because you are in their "home." At the vending machine, the washing machine, or even in the lounge and study areas. Of course, some people will look at you like you're crazy, but it's more likely to go better than just walking up to people on campus and asking them if they would live in eternal glory with Jesus if they were to die today. It's the law of averages; you want to reach out in the areas you have the greatest opportunity for impact.

To be extremely frank, that is where you will find most of the sin taking place on campus. Numbers of people will engage in fornication in residence halls all over the country tonight. There will no doubt be massive amounts of drunken co-eds in those same places. Rape, suicide, and drug use will all happen perpetually unless someone who carries this glorious gospel steps forward. The residence halls are usually the front lines in the battle over the heart of the campus. All of the organizations and even the school faculty will use the halls to communicate important information.

It's a refreshing thought that people are typically themselves when they are "home." (I put home in quotes because it's not really home but it serves as one for months out of the year.)

If they lie, they will probably not hesitate to lie at home. If the swear profusely, then guess what will come forth. When they are vulnerable, guess where they are most likely to show it? When the emptiness of countless drunken nights, shallow sexual encounters, and the pressures of the world come crashing in, who will be the sounding board? This is a chance for God's people to show true care and hope. Care is the key. I am not talking about cold calculated false care to get a proverbial spiritual notch on your belt. This has everything to do with real care for others and their current standing before a Holy God. We should be moved with compassion for those around us. This book's goal is to help you build strategic opportunities and be a voice for that cause.

Attractive

Are you an option for others? Honestly, do people know you exist, and do they come to you when they are in need, hurting, or overcome with joy? Are you attractive? The Bible says,

> "Do everything readily and cheerfully—no bickering, no second-guessing allowed! Go out into the world uncorrupted, a breath of fresh air in this squalid and polluted society. Provide people with a glimpse of good living and of the living God."
>
> Philippians 2:14–15 (Message)

Doesn't that kind of person sound attractive? Are you a breath of fresh air for those who live around you, or are you just another face in the crowd? We are to be an example to others of what it looks like to follow Jesus. I don't know what that looks like through your personality. I can tell you that those on your campus will notice when you start to shine in this way. They will become moths seeking the flame of the love of God; they may not even know why. Now when they get to you, you should have something to say.

Let's look at some ways you can radiate your light more fully. One area is prayer. We discussed prayer earlier, but you really can make a difference on your campus through your prayers. You can offer prayer to your roommates. Yes, they may be resistant and think you are out of your mind. But, I have never seen anyone in crisis refuse prayer. When they are struggling with their grades, they are open to your prayers. When their relationships are falling apart, that prayer you offered looks very attractive. If a loved one dies, your door will probably be the first on which they knock. This does not mean that you need their permission to pray in secret, but this is a way to make yourself available to them.

Another way is to serve people. Jesus said that those who would be the greatest would be the servants. Wash the dishes, sweep the floor, and clean the bathroom. Serve them. When you serve them, you do it as an offering to God, and amaze them by your diligence. You are letting your light shine, remember. I'm not just talking about cleaning up after yourself; you're an adult so that is what is expected. Even though many college students' rooms are a mess, when you keep your room clean and assist them, that's powerful. Serve hard. That will seem so strange to people who aren't walking with

Jesus. Actually, that will seem strange to people walking with Him, too!

We are in such a "me" focused society that this is completely counter-cultural. Actually, it's human nature to want others to serve us and not want to serve them. Look at what Jesus told His disciples.

> "...Whoever wants to become great among you must be your servant, and whoever wants to be first must be slave of all. For even the Son of Man did not come to be served, but to serve, and to give his life as a ransom for many."
>
> Mark 10:43–45 (NIV)

We are to serve others, sacrificially. The biggest issue you will face doing this is getting over your own pride. "I am not cleaning up someone else's mess." That statement just may hide our light from people who desperately need to see it. It's completely strange and different, but that is why it's effective. Yes, they will probably try to take advantage of you and use it to their benefit. That's why many people won't even try this, but the rewards are great. This is radical I know, but if you serve your suite mates and your neighbors, you will glow. Believe me! There was a guy I went to school with who lived like this. He was a Christian and was just a simple guy who worked hard and was very pleasant. He would come to our hall prayer meeting and would just go about his day as any other student. He was really a nice guy. One night someone made a big mess in the hallway, and he was blamed for it. He argued that he didn't do it, and honestly it wasn't in his character. Instead of continuing the argument, he in humility cleaned the mess. A month or so later while on Christmas break, this young man died in a car accident. At his memorial, someone told the story of how he had cleaned the hall, when he was innocent. It was a simple act of service that lived beyond this young man's life. That is letting your light shine. Serve them, and they just may come!

You have to learn to use what you have and who you are to attract people. Do you love movies? How about having a free movie night in you room or suite. That will not cost you much and people just may come. How's your cooking? If you are gifted in the culinary arts, then you may want to take one night a month and cook your best meal. Then open your door and watch people follow the aroma down the hall and into your room. Here's a secret I learned many years ago about college students. If you feed them, they will come. Imagine your whole hall at your room begging for food. Yes, it may cost you a little money, but the person that you may get to know may see Jesus in you and choose Him as their Savior. Can you put a price on that? That price has been paid in full by the blood of the cross. These suggestions may seem radical because they will bring attention to you. That's only a bad thing when you want all the attention for yourself and don't deflect it toward Christ.

The possibilities are endless for reaching your campus housing community. You are limited by your own imagination. The question you must ask yourself is how creative and strategic can you be. I gave you a few suggestions, which are by no means an exhaustive list, but I hope this sparks you in the way you see evangelist opportunities in residential housing from a resident's perspective.

Resident Advisor

Whether your school calls them resident advisors, resident assistants, or community assistants, they are people in the resident halls who are responsible for keeping order and adding support to students. These positions are great places of influence and impact for Christ's sake. You can make a major difference in the lives of others around you by strategically assuming this role. Many people are content to leave the hard work for someone else, but the agenda for your residential facility is being set by someone. You will have a chance to be a part of it. So, why not be the one who sets the standard?

Let's consider for instance that most Resident Assistants (RAs) are usually allowed into the halls before everyone else is allowed to enter. This is a great opportunity to go in before the others students arrive and pray. Pray for them to develop a love relationship with Jesus. Pray for their school year, families, majors, etc. Pray! There is usually a list of student's names with room assignments. This gives you a chance to pray for people by name before you ever officially meet. How powerful is that! This position is one that will afford you some amazing moments to touch the lives of others.

Often RAs will be asked to put on programs for their residence. If your campus is having a rise in suicide, you can welcome a psycho therapist in to discuss depression and related issues. Basically, you can meet the very real needs of those around you. You can stimulate conversations that lead people one step closer to Jesus.

There are usually no rules saying that the person can't be a Christian. This may give you a chance to invite your college pastor in to discuss relevant spiritual or character issues. This opens the door for you to potentially welcome professionals from your church and the community to speak to the students. This doesn't have to be your goal. It's just one way to leverage your influence. But, you don't even have to feel like you have to preach to people with every program. You can get people to think about their lives and the direction in which they are headed. You can challenge people to make better choices with their life.

We as followers of Christ can fall victim to the mindset that we are ineffective if we don't have people make a commitment to Christ when we want them to. They have to make a journey the same as you did. Your job is to plant seeds of righteousness. You may be watering a seed that was planted by some youth pastor or through the prayer of godly parents. Look at the words of Paul...

> "So then neither he who plants is anything, nor he who waters, but God who gives the increase. Now he who plants and he who waters are one, and each one will receive his own reward according to his own labor."
>
> 1 Corinthians 3:7–8 (NKJV)

By planting seeds that make people consider their lives, you will make a difference! If those in your residential facility seem to be scatterbrained and unable to maintain order in their lives, then you may want to bring in a time management specialist. If there are a lot of crimes happening at your school, you may want bring in a public safety expert. What are the needs on your campus? All schools have to, by law, make available public safety information. Look to that information to get some campus needs and create some learning opportunities. (This also works through chartered organizations, but we will go through that information later.) If there is a high rate of sexually transmitted diseases at your school, then ask a physician to speak to your building. Meet the need!

This is not to say that you can have decidedly Christian-themed programs as a residential advisor. When I was in school, the "religious" types of programs were not an issue. So, one of my many events was a midnight prayer. It was so successful that other halls started holding prayer and, on any given night, hundreds of people could be praying and learning from the Bible. It started a revolution and changed the culture of the school for several years. People would come out in record numbers around exam times, and some would stay after to receive Christ for the first time. We experienced a move of God on our campus, and it was being facilitated through students serving in the housing department.

Caution: If you are selfish, then the
resident assistant position is not for you.

It will require a great deal of your time and effort. It's a job filled with inconvenience and discomfort. But, many first year students will remember their "RAs" for the rest of their lives. You can leave an imprint on a student that will never be erased. When they are in crisis over grades, you can be there. When someone is in need of a kind word, you can speak up. When people are wrestling with character issues and in trouble over misconduct in the facility, you can be a voice of correction and encouragement. To be in someone's life and possibly make that kind of a difference is priceless.

To add to the spiritual opportunities that are available as a resident advisor, there are sometimes several natural benefits also. Most schools have some kind of incentives for opting to take the position. Some colleges pay for your living accommodations. Others will give you a stipend that can help take care of some basic needs. Others will cover your meal plan. I have heard of several schools that will pay for all of the above. It's a win/win situation. You can reach out to people with the love of Christ and benefit financially. That's a good thing. It's worthwhile just for the spiritual opportunities, but when you add it all together, I wonder why more believers don't apply for these jobs. The harvest is plentiful, and housing is a great place to reap the benefits.

Off Campus

If you are a student that lives off campus, you have some opportunities also. Some people are not made for the on-campus living experience. Don't feel left out if you are one to add mileage to you school expenses. There are several schools in which there are no residence halls and all students commute.

God can use your situation as well. The key is to make the most of your college living experience.

Interestingly enough, many commuter students live in off campus apartments where other students have a tendency to live. Many apartment complex owners choose to buy near campuses for that reason. They know that every year a whole new crop of students will be in search of affordable housing. You can build community right where you are. Since people don't feel so forced to live in sync with others, this will often take a little more creativity and strategy, but it is still possible. The key for you may be creating community within your complex, which is the automatic benefit of living on campus. You may have to think of ways to do that in your context.

You may want to consider having a Bible study. Bible studies are great tools for spreading the message of the Good News. Just make sure you know what you are talking about. People, especially unbelievers, will come with questions, and you want to at least have some answers. Another option for outreach is to create a carpooling group from your apartment to campus. This will give you a window of time in which you can be a voice for Christ. People become very friendly when they don't have a choice. Out of the time spent in the car, you may make a new friend and hopefully shine your light in such a way that they may consider listening to the gospel. Once again, all of the suggestions in this book may not work for your campus or your personality. The bottom line is that you have been sent by God to display His Glory to the world. You will probably have greater success at your mission if you think strategically and move intentionally.

ON TOP OF
ORGANIZATIONS

There are more places for Kingdom impact on your campus than you know. The chartered organizations are a great place to touch lives for Christ. Most campuses have organizations whose sole purpose is to serve the holistic needs of students. Look at your school's website for a moment and check out all the different groups meeting on your campus. Some may be official and others may not, but people are longing to belong. Even the outcast groups usually congregate together. We are made to be communal beings, so we have a habit of gravitating to others with like personalities, interests, and passions. Some choose the Greek societies, and others find a home in ethnically-centered associations. We all want to feel loved and supported. If you can work with an organization and leverage your life for Jesus, you just may be used as a powerful tool against the enemy.

We previously investigated the areas you are most passionate about, and that is a good place to start when searching for the group with which to get involved. If you love community service, connect with those on your campus who share your interest. I love community service because you can reach a broad spectrum of people that way. People can be very resistant to the gospel, but they will be wide open to help a children's shelter or feed the homeless. Not only atheists and agnostics, but good wholesome Muslims and Buddhists want to serve the community too. You could have access to people who you may never come across otherwise.

In doing community service, you not only can be a resource for those to whom you are serving, but you also are adjusting some people's perspectives about Christians. We are occasionally viewed as people who love to talk about God and not help people in distress in the name of God. Sadly, this is true for some who say they carry Christ's name. You now, through service, get a chance to show them what real life in Christ looks like.

"Anyone who sets himself up as "religious" by talking a good game is self-deceived. This kind of religion is hot air and only hot air. Real religion, the kind that passes muster before God the Father, is this: Reach out to the homeless

and loveless in their plight, and guard against
corruption from the godless world."

James 1:26–27 (The Message)

There are many Christian people filled with hot air. This is
not to condemn those who name the name of Christ, but rather
an admission of our failure to display God's Glory. Real life
in Christ has service as an immediate product. Can we blame
those who don't walk with Jesus for pointing out this flaw in
our collective character? Yes, there are many who understand
this critical spiritual principal and walk it out daily. But some
of our brothers and sisters are only focused on themselves. All
you can do is make sure that you live the life God has called
you to live.

Service presents itself in many ways. As a resident assistant
and a campus ministry leader, I leveraged both to create a
midnight prayer on campus. At the end of the school year, we
won my school's service award for serving our campus through
prayer. This was usually an award given to either service organizations or Greek organizations. This was the first time that
anyone could remember that a Christian organization won. I
didn't attend a Christian school, but they still noticed the service inherent within prayer. That's impact! You have areas in
which you can serve your campus whether or not you serve in
a service-focused group. The advantage in a service organization is that you are working with and often for people you can
evangelize.

I encourage you not to only to work in service-based organizations but to also find a place of influence within them if

possible. You're called to shine. That means that you will and should lead whenever the opportunity presents itself, not necessarily as the main person, but as a critical participant. You may be the one who is to lead the whole thing, and if you are, lead people in a way that they feel as if Jesus himself were there leading. Don't run from those opportunities when they come; embrace them. If you are more likely to lead from the background, then do it with all you have. The bottom line is to leverage your influence.

Chartered Organizations

When looking at the different types of organizations on your campus, there are probably many groups with varying focuses. Chartered organizations have a tendency to come in all sizes, shapes and colors. Some get funds from student fees, and others don't. It will serve you well to find one that suits your particular needs and desires. If you are Asian, and interested connecting with other Asians, then use that as a window into the lives of others. If you are studying medicine and there is a health-based organization, get involved. Just make sure that your commitment to the organization doesn't get in the way of your commitment to Christ. The group with which you align yourself should be used for you to display Him. This can happen by your choosing to be an advocate for God-honoring projects or by your just letting your light shine through relationships.

It's a good thing to find what sparks you and get involved. Join the future business leader's organization. If that is where your passions lie, go for it. Organizations are not only for community service. Yes, you should be helping others who cannot help themselves, and that can be accomplished off campus through churches and not-for-profit organizations. But, it is not a sin to be in a group that values social activities. The barometer is whether or not what the group is doing will allow you to obey God's Word. If so, then enjoy yourself. If any organization would cause you to compromise your spiritual beliefs, then leave it alone.

There are fantastic networking opportunities that are created in social environments that will help you accomplish God's plans in your life. Not to mention the chance to have plain old fashioned fun. Yes, the "F" word. You should enjoy your collegiate experience and make the most of it.

Chartered organizations can be great places to build friendships and connections with people who you will value for the rest of your life. We will look at campus ministries later in this chapter because they provide some important opportunities also. But, you should not be so entrenched in any organization that you are nonexistent in your classes. You are called to make a difference on your campus, and you must be engaged in the lives of those who don't know Christ for His sake. The interesting thing is that many Christians may not understand why you would choose to spend time with the non-Christians. That is not a concern when you are rooted and grounded in a living faith in Jesus.

It's true that you are either influencing others or you are being influenced by them. So, it's paramount that you make sure you are not being dragged down. Jesus shows us how to tow that line.

"Then Jesus went again to walk alongside the
lake. Again a crowd came to him, and he taught
them. Strolling along, he saw Levi (Matthew),
son of Alphaeus, at his work collecting taxes.
Jesus said, "Come along with me." He came.
Later Jesus and his disciples were at home having supper with a collection of disreputable
guests. Unlikely as it seems, more than a few of
them had become followers. The religion scholars and Pharisees saw him keeping this kind of
company and lit into his disciples: "What kind
of example is this, acting cozy with the riffraff?"
Jesus, overhearing, shot back, "Who needs a
doctor: the healthy or the sick? I'm here inviting the sin-sick, not the spiritually-fit."

Mark 2:13–17 (Message)

We see in this scripture a reflection of what I think is many
collegiate Christians' struggle. It's easy to want to stay in a safe
place and connect with the only believers on the campus. That
keeps you out of trouble, right? Yes. But, it doesn't give you
the opportunity to start any trouble either. Jesus was a bit of a
trouble maker Himself, and we are to follow His example. The
spiritual leadership of His day thought He had lost His mind.
Why would a spiritual person hang with a bunch of crooks and
sinners? To reach them!

It should be the story of Christians that everyone that hangs
around us becomes Christians or at least steps closer to Christ.
This is a radical way of living, but I believe if more people

lived like this the world would be different. Sadly, the opposite occurs more frequently than many want to admit. I believe it is a difference in mindsets. It's the difference between conforming to the world and conquering the world. In my years serving college students, I have discovered that the students who are more focused on "staying saved" are the ones who often walk away from Christ. The ones who are committed to taking over are the ones who ultimately make it.

> *Caution: Some will blur the lines between impacting the world and friendship with the world.*

I have seen it numerous times. Some students in the name of "reaching others" will begin to live in such a way that others are incapable of distinguishing whether or not they know Jesus at all. This happens when students are either unaware of their own susceptibility to sin or when they secretly desire the pleasures of this world more than the glorious life in Christ. Both are just as dangerous.

> "You adulterous people, don't you know that friendship with the world is hatred toward God? Anyone who chooses to be a friend of the world becomes an enemy of God."
>
> James 4:4(NIV)

A remedy for your own ignorance to your weaknesses is that you must embrace your own depravity. The Bible encourages us to be careful not to think more highly of ourselves then we ought. We all are vulnerable to temptation! When you can admit your weaknesses, then you can ask God for the strength to overcome in those areas. It's also necessary not to thirst for the pleasures of this world. Whether you have been in church all your life, or are a new convert, our bodies lust for things that are displeasing to God. We have to fight those desires through prayer, the reading of scripture, and through accountability with other believers. You must continually take inventory of your own desires if you are going to befriend those who are in need of Christ. That is not to scare you away from inviting non-Christians into your life; it's an encouragement to remain dependant on God and other believers in the process.

Greek Life

There is no way to discuss college organizations and not at least spend some time on Greek life. The subject of Fraternities and Sororities is often a hot button issue in the realm of college ministry. I am often asked by students if it's good for a Christian to pledge a Greek letter organization. So we will spend some time going through that decision. Before we get into the topic, it's important to note that Greek letter organizations vary. For example, African Americans have nine of their own historically black fraternities and sororities that are not connected to the mainstream organizations. Within all Greek organizations, the rules, rituals, and goals are often different. This is not a specific breakdown of all Greek letter organizations and their practices, but rather a way to determine whether or not one is a fit for you as a Christian.

My first encouragement is to look into what the organization stands for. If it's a service organization, then see what services they offer. There are some that tout service, but they are really a social group. Even if an organization says that they were founded on Christian principles, make sure that they adhere to those principles. Also, make sure you know what you are getting yourself into and count the cost of your commitment. When you know what you believe, it's easy to weed out groups that don't align with your faith.

If an organization says they have been founded on Christian principles, it's possible that the whole organization may have had some fundamental changes that impact how it functions. You must also look at under whom you will be pledging. The national organization may have bylaws that the local chapter may not follow. Do your research! I wouldn't encourage anyone to join a business organization that they could not research. You want to ensure that what you commit yourself to does not conflict with the God to whom you have committed your entire being.

Based on those criteria alone you can determine whether or not becoming Greek is a worthwhile endeavor. You have to work it out through prayer, serious contemplation and research to know if this is a good move for you. Why would I say that about Greek letter groups and not other chartered organizations? It's because these organizations ask for often lifetime commitment. Most non-Greek groups will take you for a semester or maybe even expect participation for the duration of your collegiate life. There is often a more selective process to join a Fraternity or Sorority. Since they usually

require a greater commitment, it's wise to take greater inventory
before joining.

---

*Caution: You should never join a Greek
organization because your friend, mentor, or parent(s) were apart of it.*

It's completely normal to be drawn toward a particular group
based on your connection to it through someone else. That is
natural and not in itself a bad thing. But, you may not fully
know the reasons they joined the organization or their spiritual
condition while deciding. This decision must be yours! You
are the one who will have to live with the benefits and/or the
consequences of your decision.

There can be some great opportunities for friendship and
evangelism in Greek organizations. One of my students began
a Bible study amongst her sorority members. Another became
a spiritual mentor to those who pledged after her. Some local
chapters have been havens for spiritual growth and development. If you are already a part of one of these groups, then
shine for Christ! If you are considering becoming a member,
then make sure it's an environment in which you can shine!

As a college minister, I must also bring some focus to an
ugly side of the pledging process. Depending on your organization's bylaws, for those under whom you will pledge and/
or the school you attend, hazing can be a serious issue. Most
national Greek offices condemn the practice of hazing, but
sadly it persists. Things like binge drinking, severe paddling,
and sleep depravation have resulted in serious injuries and even

death. This is always unacceptable! If you are in an organization and this is happening, you have the power to stop it. If
you are being abused while "on line," then please inform your
pastor or ministry leader. No one has the right to abuse you or
anyone else.

What do you do if you are on line and you are noticing
unbiblical treatment or requirements? I encourage you to pro-
test, and if need be, drop from pledging. I know this can be
difficult, but if you are being forced to do something that is
against your beliefs, then you must side with Christ above all
else. For example, if you are being forced to binge drink, the
Bible says...

"Don't destroy yourself by getting drunk, but
let the Spirit fill your life."
Ephesians 5:18 (CEV)

If it comes down to your obedience to the Bible or to the
organization, then always side with the Bible. Some may say
that this is in the most extreme of circumstances, and yes that
is true. But, I know people who have had to stop pledging
because of these types of conflicts. I know others who were
beaten and refused to continue on with the process. The truth
is these things happen, and I want to make you protect your
testimony and your life if necessary. Once again if the Greek
organization passes all of the spiritual criteria, then enjoy yourself and let your light shine.

Campus Ministries

Campus ministries are a wonderful way to engage in campus outreach, fellowship, and worship opportunities. There are many national and local campus ministries that have held up the banner for Christ in powerful ways. I used to work for a national college ministry, so I see the need for campus-based Christian groups. I encourage as many students as possible to get involved with a campus ministry. It would be good to know how many Christian Ministries there are on your campus. It's encouraging to know who else is intentionally committing their lives to making a difference for Christ on your campus.

Knowing who else is there serves at least two important functions. First, it gives you an opportunity to pray for them. The Bible says...

> "And pray in the Spirit on all occasions with all kinds of prayers and requests. With this in mind, be alert and always keep on praying for all the saints."
>
> Ephesians 6:18 (NIV)

Pray for the others who want to see God glorified on your campus. Yes, they may have a completely different philosophy of ministry. Their doctrine may not totally match yours, but they are still a part of the Kingdom of God. They are your brothers and sisters in Christ and are in need of spiritual guides and support just as you are. You might be surprised at how fast God will bless your ministry if you decide to uplift others in prayer. In all honesty, does it really matter who God uses on your campus as long as He is revealed? If he chooses to use one of the athletic campus groups, praise God! If He uses a church-based campus ministry, phenomenal! As long as at the end of the day more people come to follow Christ, then great.

The second function knowing other campus ministries accomplishes is it allows you to build a sense of connection and family amongst the believers on campus. I am not simply talking about a "unity" meeting. I know of times when it was very good to have a "unity service" and others where it was honestly a waste of time and energy. I am talking about friendships that surpass ministry meeting times. Out of basic friendships between Christians on campus more meaningful "unity" times may emerge from authentic relationships.

Sadly, many campus ministries operate like churches and compete for members and nights of worship. This is wrong, always. Our competition is not with other believers, but we are battling the devil over the souls of people who don't know God. If one group wants to meet on a particular night, then choose another to give people options. If one group has worship as a mainstay of their night, then you can focus on Bible study. If there is room for multiple Bible studies then fine, but the battle over pre-existing Christians is nonsensical. Support others' events. If you meet someone who is not a great fit for your style of ministry, then send them to another.

One scripture that I love that pertains to getting along with other ministries is Mark 9:49–50, and it reads…

"John answered, "Master, we saw someone casting out demons in your name, and we tried to
stop him, because he does not follow with us."
But Jesus said to him, "Do not stop him, for the
one who is not against you is for you." (ESV)

Whoever is not against Christ is for Him. This a good gauge
to use when considering connecting with a particular ministry.
Yes, styles change and not every spiritual event on campus is
for you. But, we should not be competing with one another
over trivial things that won't matter ultimately. I understand
that not every believer has sound doctrine. While in school, I
saw many Christian groups whose take on scripture is one in
which I was not in agreement. But, the thing is I saw God use
them also. If they are not against us, then they are with us, no
matter how much you may disagree with them. Only in the
most extreme of cases is this not true.

Caution: There are some who use Jesus'
name but they are far from Him.

There are cultish groups that claim Christ, but are anti-any
other believers that are not of their sect. I will never forget
when I was in my first year and a group such as this was very
prominent on campus. I had a discussion with a gentleman
(I use this term loosely) from their group. He proceeded to
question me on matters of faith which didn't bother me because
I knew what I believed. It was apparent that his doctrine was
way out there. I explained to him that I had confessed Jesus

as my personal savior, I was baptized to outwardly show my commitment to Jesus, I was not ashamed to be a witness for Christ, and I was even faithfully serving in my local church. That should have quieted all speculations about my salvation.

He told me that I needed to be baptized in His church in order to be "saved." I continued to share how Christ had change my life, and he responded with, "I don't know who changed your life but it sure wasn't Jesus." His group was later banned from campus for pursuing people so dogmatically that they literally gave people mental breakdowns. From groups such as this, it's good to keep your distance.

One major issue with ministries on campus is they can become cliquish. I have seen and been a part of groups like this. The interesting thing is most Christian cliques don't know that they are in fact cliques. Christian ministries don't usually start by saying, "We are going to be a clique, and no new people allowed." Most of them simply feel a strong sense of connection to the overall group, which is not bad at all. Here are some ways to see if a particular ministry has become a clique.

Everyone in the group is pretty much the same. Same general background, general interest, and cultural context.

Everyone spends time with the same group with few if any friends that are not a part of the group.

It's difficult for anyone to join the group, especially if they don't come from the same background.

People feel a strange sense of discomfort when they get around existing members.

All of the jokes are "inside jokes", and all the references come with a "you had to be there."

If you answered yes to any of the above, there is a chance your group may have gone from a ministry to a clique. Like I stated earlier, I have made this mistake also. It's natural to want to exist in a caring and nurturing environment. Our friends should serve as a support base for us. But, when we take our eyes off of the mission field God has laid before us, we are missing the mark as a ministry. Yes, a ministry should be as one. That is one of its major purposes. When an organization goes from reaching to fellowshipping only, that is a travesty. The converse is just as true. We can sometimes exist in ministry constructs that are completely focused on others. It should not be an either/or decision, but rather both/and. The great commission and the great commandment work in conjunction to make us all that God has for us.

If you don't spend time with those who don't know Christ, how will they get to know Him through you? You can't just hang out with Christians all the time. That is a church youth group mentality (I have nothing against youth groups, by the way). Many youth and college ministers are so busy trying to keep people saved, that they never challenge them to imagine taking over. Jesus faced a similar situation as we saw in Mark Chapter 2. The religious leaders of His day didn't understand how He could spend so much time with sinners. A campus ministry should build authentic community with its members and help launch them into the campus.

DISCIPLESHIP
DILEMMA

The question was asked earlier if it would matter that you were ever on your campus. That is a question that will continually need to be answered as you matriculate. There is one way to ensure that you leave a spiritual legacy on you campus: mentor someone who will be there when you leave. Discipleship is simply replicating oneself. It's all about replacing your impact with someone(s) who sees things similarly as you. This doesn't mean the person will be just like you, but rather they have some of the spiritual DNA that allows you to be who you are and do what you do. The truth is that people are going to follow someone. Why not you? That is, if you have decided to follow Christ with all you have and make an impact for Him.

First, you have to know that you are someone who God can use as a model of His life on campus. This doesn't mean that you must have it all together; I don't know anyone who does. It means that, to the best of your ability, you are living for Jesus. Yes, you may sin from time to time, but your heart should be to please Him. Think about it. If you consider yourself a "weak" Christian and everyone else on your campus who is not saved was like you, the campus would still be better, because they would still be Christians. That is a message of hope.

You may need to recalibrate your perception of discipleship also. We think of discipleship as one older Christian taking a younger Christian on as a spiritual growth project. That is not the total picture painted by Christ. Look at how He welcomed people to follow him. "Come and see," and, "Follow me," were the requirements for discipleship. We see the Savior taking a vastly different approach than we sometimes see today. He grabbed a bunch of unlikely guys to do the work of spreading the Good News. The requirement to follow you should be a simple willingness.

> "As Jesus passed on from there, He saw a man named Matthew sitting at the tax collector's office; and He said to him, Be My disciple [side with My party and follow Me]. And he rose and followed Him. And as Jesus reclined at table in the house, behold, many tax collectors

and [especially wicked] sinners came and sat
(reclined) with Him and His disciples."

Matthew 9:9–10 (Amplified Bible)

Matthew was a pretty crooked guy, and he simply received an
invitation to follow Christ. He then, in turn, invited His friend
over to meet Jesus. That's Discipleship. Yes, there is room for
mature believers to mentor immature ones. But, we see Jesus
welcoming people who others would think were unworthy to
be associated with Him. We have the same opportunities to
welcome unbelieving people into our world.

The hard part is that it's hard to manage their behavior.
These disciples have a tendency to not act as good wholesome
Christians. They may make you look bad. So what! Unbelievers
don't usually act like believers until they become believers.
Then, it still may take a while. You need only look at your
behavior since embracing Jesus to see that. Let them come!
Only Christ can change a heart. It took Jesus three years, dying
on a cross, and rising again to finally reach those guys, and
Judas didn't make it. There are no quick fixes when it comes to
helping someone develop a solid life in Christ. In spite of that,
your request should be come and see my life, flaws and all.

Attracting Disciples

I have heard it said in several different ways. "If you call
yourself a leader, and no one is following, then you're just
taking a walk." I think this is true for a few reasons, but one
major one is that we don't know how to recruit. **Jesus was
sought out by some, and He went after others.** It's important

to do both if we are going to have people to pour our lives into. It's been my experience that you will have to invite many more than will seek you out, but you must have eyes to see potential and a heart to accept new people that are drawn to your light.

Let's look at Jesus' example of recruiting disciples in scripture.

> "The next day John was there again with two of his disciples. When he saw Jesus passing by, he said, "Look, the Lamb of God!" When the two disciples heard him say this, they followed Jesus. Turning around, Jesus saw them following and asked, "What do you want?" They said, "Rabbi" (which means Teacher), "where are you staying?" "Come," he replied, "and you will see." So they went and saw where he was staying, and spent that day with him. It was about the tenth hour.
>
> Andrew, Simon Peter's brother, was one of the two who heard what John had said and who had followed Jesus. The first thing Andrew did was to find his brother Simon and tell him, "We have found the Messiah" (that is, the Christ). And he brought him to Jesus. Jesus looked at him and said, "You are Simon son of John. You will be called Cephas" (which, when translated, is Peter). The next day Jesus decided to leave for Galilee. Finding Philip, he said to him, "Follow me.""
>
> John 1:35–43 (NIV)

The day after Jesus was baptized by John, John points out who Jesus was. Andrew then went and spent the day with Jesus and was so convinced that he was the Messiah that he went and got Peter his brother. Although this text does not spell it out, we know from the other gospels that after meeting Andrew and Peter, Jesus performed a miracle before their eyes with fish, for that was their occupation. Then, before leaving the area Jesus welcomes James, John, and Phillip to be His disciples.

So let's map out how Jesus attracted his disciples.

- He was talked about by John so much that Andrew sought Jesus out.

- Then Jesus welcomed Andrew to spend the day with Him.

- Andrew introduces Peter and Jesus.

- Then Jesus seeks them out at their job.

- Jesus then invites James and John.

- Jesus also finds Phillip and welcomes Him into His story.

The point is that Jesus both invited people in whom He saw potential and welcomed those who were interested in getting to know Him. Please pay attention to the fact that Jesus did more pursuing of them than they did of Him. I mention that because John tells us that He is the Light of the World. If He, being The Light, had to go after His Disciples, then don't think that masses of people will come to you because you have your little light shining. You must at times go out to make disciples. This is in no way to minimize your significance as a light bearer, but rather a call to go after people who won't come unless you bid them.

Discipleship Takes Time

When you look at your campus impact, you want to make sure you are leaving a Godly legacy. You will have to work for that legacy just as Christ did His. This is viewed as unnecessary by some. It's thought that people will just come because you exist. I don't understand that perspective when Jesus is our example. I believe in basic evangelistic discipleship. It causes you to take risks on people the same way God took risks on us.

I do believe that people will be drawn to your light as a follower of Christ. There will be people who will live in your residence hall, see you in class, or just see you about your daily schedule that will see a difference in you. That should be the case. But, others may not recognize where your light comes from or know how to ask you about it. Still others because of selfishness or spiritual blindness may not see it at all. That's why you will have to befriend people, see where they are spiritually and strategically invite them into your life. If all Christians had to do was show up, then the world would have been saved by now.

We have to, with the greatest authenticity, befriend people to disciple them. We discussed ways to gain entry points into people's lives in earlier chapters. But, when it comes to mentoring it takes more work. Individuals can't feel as if you are taking them on as a project. They are people. Yes, you should want them to come to the knowledge of the truth, but you should care for them as Christ cares and not with the intention to add an additional notch to your spiritual belt. Quick, loud, and big only usually works in short-term situations. For example, if you are doing a special event, or if there is a major immediate concern on your campus, you can usually expect people to be drawn in large moments. But true discipleship will take time.

You may not even want to call it discipleship. A better word may be mentoring. Christians like to say disciple because it means something to us. If you are developing relationships with unbelievers, they may not take too kindly to being called your disciple. The key is to start with people where they are, and it may mean you may have to adjust your schedule to accommodate them instead of the other way around. You may have to abandon Christian jargon until they understand what you're talking about.

Many Christians expect more from those coming to investigate Jesus than we do people who say they follow Him. People will come cursing and fornicating and God knows what else. But, what else do you expect? They are being themselves, and all they ask of you is that you be yourself. It's only over time that we start to see behaviors changing. You must make up in your mind that you are willing to work with people long enough for them to have a true encounter with Christ. If you bail on them, then where does the hope come from?

Making Disciples

This type of discipleship usually doesn't begin in a church building (although it can). It happens at the coffee shop or over study notes. This is the process of allowing someone else to grab a hold on your life. Yes, there is a weight attached to it. You are now their Christian experience until they develop a vibrant walk with Christ for themselves, so you have to walk carefully. When you do make mistakes, be honest about it, apologize and move on. Remember, you are not meant to be an example of perfect living, but that of perfect grace.

This should be a progressive process. People should not remain at the introductory stages of faith forever. Over time, Jesus required increased commitment of those who followed him. He started with a follow me, but He turned the heat up on those closest to Him.

> "If you want to be my disciple, you must hate everyone else by comparison—your father and mother, wife and children, brothers and sisters—yes, even your own life. Otherwise, you cannot be my disciple."
>
> Luke 14:26 (NLT)

Jesus got tough with those who had been traveling with him for a while. Likewise, you must wisely look for opportunities to challenge people in their commitment to Christ. It may start with casual conversation, become a genuine friendship, but at some point you need to find out about their spiritual condition and give them a chance to see yours. Once you have earned their trust and respect, then you have an open window to have deep and sometimes uncomfortable conversation. This comes at different times for each person. It takes a sensitive heart and wise timing to do this effectively, but God will guide you if you let him.

To be honest, it took me a while to learn the ebbs and flows of this type of discipleship. My roommate in college is a positive story of how this works. We didn't start out sharing a room together. We actually met over a heaping pile of disgusting cafeteria food. He wasn't a Christian at the time. It kind of went like this...

—Hey.

> Hi.

—Are you getting settled?

> Yeah, I guess. I am just looking
> at all these beautiful women around
> here. I love this place. And you?

—I am here for school and for God's purpose, I don't have time to look at the girls. (I thought it was the spiritual thing to say).

> You're crazy! All these women here,
> and you are talking God stuff. I believe
> in God, but I will have to think about
> that stuff later.

He was a Christian by the end of the semester. We later became roommates and made a great impact together. We still laugh at that conversation to this day. Now, that was God's timing and dumb luck (not that I believe in luck). But, I stumbled into that. It may happen where you accidentally connect with someone, like I did. All you can do is work with the opportunities God gives you. He used my overly "religious" response to open a door for real conversation.

On the other hand, I have ruined it just as easily. There was a young lady that had recently become a part of the campus ministry I led. She was in her first year and had come from a church with a strong youth group. I made my first mistake by assuming she was more spiritual than she actually was because she came from a good church background. I began to require (as if I had that authority) her presence at Morning Prayer at 6:30 a.m. She made it to a couple. I was insistent that if she was really serious about her walk with Jesus she would be there. Then I told her she needed to come to our evening programs and serve at our fundraisers. Let's just say that by the second semester, she didn't even look in my direction. I was the devil in her eyes. I blew it!

It's because I was expecting her to match my commitment when she was just deciding if this "Jesus Thing" was for her. I now wish I could get those moments back. She needed a friend, and I was a drill sergeant. I required too much too soon, and she ran for her life. I can now only pray that she eventually found a mature believer that would lovingly walk her to the cross of Christ. I wish I could say she was the only person I pushed either too fast or too slow. But, I learned over time to walk at the pace that others can handle. It's our job to create the opportunity for people to be disciples, not to do the job that only God can. Open your heart to people and follow God, and people will follow you.

Mentoring Other Christians

Mentoring Christians is the side of discipleship we are more used to. It is just as critical on campuses across the country as evangelistic discipleship. This is especially true when you consider that roughly 80% of high schools' "Christians" no longer follow Jesus upon the completion of college. Someone needs to intentionally and strategically reach out to incoming students. Think about it, there are students all over your campus that have a good biblical foundation, but it may not have fully taken root. They are just waiting to see someone who knows how to apply those principles as a single adult. That will take compassionate leadership from someone who knows their God and is willing to inconvenience themselves for Christ.

The person who does this may have to come back to school from vacation early just to meet and get to know the incoming students. You'd be surprised how good of a glimpse into spiritual backgrounds people have just by meeting their parents. As a Resident Assistant, I had a great chance to see who had a church background. Then I would invite those students out to ministry events and to church. Now, I did that through my job, but some Fraternities and Sororities utilize the same strategy to recruit new members. It's an effective means of first contact.

You will probably run into two distinct "Christian" first year students. One group has had some significant experiences with God. They had an amazing youth ministry or had some really amazing parents as examples. The goal in connecting with this group is giving them something attractive with which to be a part. They will want to continue the walk they have began as a high school student. Then there are some itching to walk away from their church experience, faith, and any semblance of religion. They are often in search of a testimony (meaning they want to taste sin) or running from what they deem was an oppressive religious upbringing. These are the ones that you want to establish friendships with just let them know who you are and who you represent. They will know where to go when times get hard. These are generally people who have a church background, but they have no relationship with Jesus. These students are the mission field at many Christian colleges.

With Christians (or those with a Christian background) you don't necessarily need to start from the ground up when it comes to biblical principles. They are usually very familiar with the concept of the Trinity and spiritual morality. Your job will be to show them that there is a hope in living this life as a single adult. They no longer have someone telling them what to do so they are in need of a model to lead the way. Your example is exactly what is needed. That means that you can't be selfish and you have to follow Christ with all you have. Then you can proudly say, "Follow me as I follow Christ." That will even be alluring to those who are trying to escape the Christian world because many of them are looking for true believers their age. When they realize that what they assumed was life was just an illusion, they will come looking for something more.

If you are going to make a lasting impact on your campus, you must replicate yourself. It doesn't matter whether or not you feel as if you're good enough to disciple someone. If you have Jesus in your heart, you have something to give. This is not a glamorous process and it may take more time than you ever imagined, but it's worth it. Sometimes the people you will lead will be ungrateful for your time and effort. But, it is worth it!

If you make an impact on your campus in the four years of your collegiate journey, but leave no one behind to continue what you began, then you have no spiritual legacy. One of the best things you can do for the Kingdom of God is to make sure that the next group of students has an option to receive Christ because of what you have done. Discipleship is the key. Pour your life into believers and unbelievers alike, and you will be amazed with the result.

CHERISH
CHURCH

L et me first say that I love the local church. With all of its issues, the church is still a wonderful institution. Jesus did not start schools or governmental entities. He established the Church, and I am glad He did. Hopefully, you are a part of a local congregation that can care for and shepherd you adequately. If not, maybe this chapter will encourage you to take a chance on the local church.

Okay. The local church is not perfect. I concede that. I think a misconception is that when you go a local church they should have everything you need and should be without flaws. This could not be farther from the truth. Think about it. When you go to some restaurants, you have a bad experience. That doesn't mean that all restaurants or even others in that chain are bad. You may have run into the wrong server or chef on the wrong day. It's the same way with the church. You may have had a bad experience with the wrong person or caught a church at its lowest point. You may have even visited an unhealthy church. That is not representative of all congregations, all pastors, or all denominations.

Some have issues with the whole denomination concept. Basically, denominations exist for a few main reasons. One reason is that we are all different and not everyone worships the same way. Most denominations have a specific way in which they conduct service. When these churches began, they usually started because a new idea about how a church service could be done emerged, and others who agreed joined them. These separate groups usually share governance and are allied together.

Another reason for the existence of denominations is slight differences in theological perspectives. There is also a common misconception that all Christians think and agree on everything. It's just not true. People are often very serious about their emphasis of certain scriptures. The key is that all churches align with basic Christian tenants. They can be found in what is known as the Apostles Creed.

> "I believe in God the Father Almighty, maker of heaven and earth; And in Jesus Christ his only Son our Lord: who was conceived by the Holy Spirit, born of the Virgin Mary, suffered under Pontius Pilate, was crucified, dead, and buried, the third day He rose from the dead; he

ascended into heaven, and sits at the right hand of the God the Father Almighty; from thence He shall come to judge the quick and the dead. I believe in the Holy Spirit, the holy Church, the communion of saints, the forgiveness of sins, the resurrection of the body, and the life everlasting. Amen."

Caution: I would be skeptical of any church that does not agree with this statement.

There are small adjustments in this that churches make, but all healthy Christian churches agree with these tenants. In current years, more churches have connected across denominational lines because pastors realize that we are one body as the church universal. There has even been the emergence of the non-denominational churches that aren't affiliated with any of the main denominations. They are not necessarily any better or worse than any of the others. The goal is to join a church that adheres to the basics of the faith.

Why We Need the Church

God knew what we needed and He prepared something in advance to meet those needs. The Church is a place where we should get spiritual guidance. You are not so spiritual that you don't need someone to help you in your journey. If you think you are, then that shows how much you are in need of someone to lead you.

"Now these are the gifts Christ gave to the
church: the apostles, the prophets, the evangelists, and the pastors and teachers. Their
responsibility is to equip God's people to do
his work and build up the church, the body
of Christ. This will continue until we all come
to such unity in our faith and knowledge of
God's Son that we will be mature in the Lord,
measuring up to the full and complete standard
of Christ."

Ephesians 4:11–13 (NLT)

The Lord knew we would have a tendency to go astray, so He
gave us gifts called church leadership. I have been a Christian
for many years now, and I still need people in my life to help
me become who God wants me to be. It's the job of church
leadership to prepare and mature us. I know no person that
has measured up to the full standard of Christ, so we need the
church for spiritual leadership. Friends who are believers are
good, and they can encourage us, but Jesus gave us gifts that are
to be found through the church.

We grow spiritually mature through teaching. Becoming a
part of a local church gives you the fast track on growth and
development. This happens when you submit yourself to the
teaching of those who know more than you. Face it, you don't
know everything. Neither do I. The Church allows us to be lovingly taught by people who care about us and want what's best
for us. When we embrace the Church, we embrace maturity.

We also have an opportunity to worship corporately through the local church. Yes, you can worship alone, but there is a special experience that we see in scripture that is for group worship. If you have experienced it, you know that there is often an unexplainable tangible sense of God's presence at corporate worship times. It's hard to express that to someone who has never had this amazing experience. The Bible encourages us to worship together.

> "The singers went before, the players on instruments *followed* after; Among *them were* the maidens playing timbrels. Bless God in the congregations, The Lord, from the fountain of Israel (God's People)."
>
> Psalm 68:25–26 (NKJV)

When we lift our voices in celebration in a group of believers, it impacts us as well as others. The Scriptures show that it touches the heart of God. When we choose to remove ourselves from the Church, it robs God of this precious praise that He deserves. That alone is reason enough to join a local church.

Another reason to engage in the local church is for the increase of outreach endeavors. Your personal outreach can now be added to numbers of others and impact more than you ever could by yourself. Think about all of the places you all by yourself may never go and all of the people you may never meet. When you are vitally connected in a church, you share in the blessings and overall effectiveness of that body. Instead

of the campus being your sole focus, you now have rolled the
entire community that the local church is reaching into your
sphere of influence. Every missionary the church sends and
supports, and every soul that is reached through those members you now share in.

Then you add a solid family into the equation. A local
church is a family. Just like in a natural family, you can build
warm relationships with those in your local community. It's
good to be known. You may not know every person in the
church, and you may not know the pastor directly, but you
should feel a genuine attachment to the Body. Depending
on the church size, it may take a moment to get connected,
but you can still identify and relate to the messages and/
or the people. This experience will be enhanced if you go to
Bible studies, prayer meetings, join small (cell) groups, Sunday
school, or whatever gathering times that particular church has.
Everyone wants to feel loved, and you are no exception, so
allow a local body to welcome you into their family.

One of the greatest things that comes with local church
membership is the privilege to serve. The campus allows you
to serve in a very direct way, but the local church gives you a
chance to develop your gifts and talents with the oversight of
seasoned believers. It's also a perfect laboratory to try ministries
you are interesting in, but have not attempted before. If you're
thinking about attempting a new ministry on campus, you can
build relationships with those from your church working in the
same general area and gain wisdom from mature adults. There
are some different ministry opportunities that are not available
on campus at a local church, child and senior adult care for

example. Local churches are in need of people like you who are willing to serve God by serving others. Service not only helps others it builds and develops you as well.

From Church to Campus and Back

All that you do on your campus for the glory of God should be an extension of your local church. All the recommendations and insights presented in this book are all to be done through you as a vehicle of your local church. Campus ministries are wonderful, but they are not local churches (except in those rare instances where a church is on campus). There are some Christian schools that have phenomenal chapels where you can be shepherded very well. Sadly, many secular schools have chapel resources that aren't Christ-centered. They usually cater to the wide audience of faiths that are represented on your campus and are usually unable to give you sound Biblical direction. (although I know some very Godly exceptions). On most campuses you will need to find an off-campus church that will be able to give you the guidance that Christ wants you to receive.

As amazing as you might be as a student, you are not a pastor. You can reach your entire campus for Jesus, but they are going to have to go somewhere to get greater spiritual leadership. You must send them to a church so that they can get the spiritual covering they will need to traverse the rocky challenges ahead. You should not have to feel the burden and responsibility of meeting the needs that a church should. It's not your job. You're not equipped with the resources necessary. This is not to diminish your impact, but rather to free you to be a fisher of men. Not a fish processing plant. That is reserved for the local church.

I have served many years as a college ministry leader, and I have seen many campus ministries and students attempts to create a church on campus. It works fine when a pastor/church planter or denomination is attempting to do it, but when an over zealous second-year student tries, it always ends in failure. It's amazing how many unprepared students unwittingly sabotage their effectiveness on campus by committing themselves to a job that is quite frankly beyond their current capabilities. If you are a student who feels God's leading to pastor, then you should first get the proper training and endorsement before jumping into a very difficult occupation. Until then, you can do a great work for Christ as a student.

The solution is to be the arms and legs of your church on your campus. You can go places and reach people that your church's leadership can't. Then you can invite the people you are touching to attend your church. You increase your church's outreach potential by being a leader on campus. You are not an island, but a vital link in the chain from the church to the campus.

While in school, I remember receiving a challenge to bring people to church on Sundays. I honestly felt wrong (not that anyone made me feel that way) for coming by myself. It was because I knew that in all my work on campus I could only take someone so far spiritually. Not to mention that there were numbers of people living godless lives all around me that I would feel convicted by not at least giving people the opportunity to go with me. So, I started asking people who were a part of my campus ministry to church. Those who were in my prayer group and in my Bible study were also invited. Anyone who did not attend a local church was in danger of being asked to attend church with me. I believed in the vision and mission of the local church, and I knew that commitment to Jesus without a church home was a prescription for failure.

My roommate who was now an amazing witness for Christ on campus was doing the same. We attended different churches so we would compete to see who could get the most people to church on a given Sunday. He had the advantage in that his church was within walking distance to the campus while mine wasn't. But, I received the joy of knowing Christ before he did, so we were even. We were strategic with whom we asked, and it was never overly competitive. The truth is the only prize we received was that we knew we in some way brought people closer to Christ. That was more than enough for the both of us.

I would then have leaders from different industries who attended my church come in and do programs in my residential facility. This was so effective that the residential department started asking people from my church to give seminars. They would share their business expertise, and if people wanted to talk after they were more than happy to tell them about Christ. It was amazing. The church is a resource pool for you. Not only can you bring people to the church from your school you can build a bridge from your congregation to the campus.

If you are in a fraternity or sorority, you may be able to find people at your church who are members. Then you can be a connection point from one to the others, all with the goal of spreading the Good News. You also can invite other students who are attending your church to campus Bible studies in an effort to help them increase their impact on campus. When you function like this, you make your church more effective and your school more Christ-centered one person at a time.

Choose Church

When choosing a place of worship, don't necessarily look at the size or popularity of a particular church. There are very large churches that are healthy and relatively small ones that are just as healthy. You want to make sure that the church you commit to is a good fit for you. It does not mean that a local church you're interested in will have all you want, but it should have the basics. You need a church home. Just like a pair of blue jeans, the churches in your community may not be a perfect fit, but you still need to be covered.

A Christian without a church home is contradictory. We were made to function within a church context. I think that Jesus knew what He was doing when He created the church. I know that sometimes it's difficult to find a good church. It's very possible that you may have had a bad experience with a church. That does not mean you give up on the institution. The church is one of the best and longest lasting organizations in existence, and for good reason. Churches are rehabilitation centers for broken lives. It's a place where we can come and be ourselves and heal from the barrage of arrows that are hurled at us daily.

If you have stopped going to church, start again. You don't have to be perfect to be a part of the church. You don't have to know all of the church formalities and protocols. Just go.

Non-denominational or the particular denomination in which you grew up doesn't matter. What matters is that you go and become a part. If you are unsure of which one to visit, then ask someone who seems to be enjoying their church experience. A good strategy would be to look at the lives of the Christians around you and go with someone who is growing spiritually.

*Caution: A church cannot be
completely judged based on the lives
of a few people who attend.*

Many people are still developing and may not be the best examples at the moment. If you attend a church and it does not fit you, then visit another. You may want to find a church that has a college ministry. This way you can be connected to others in your age range. The bottom line is to find a church.

If you are a member of a local church, then make sure you get involved. Support the leadership and ministries of the church. Your love for the local church will increase based on your service in the local church. It is also the place where you will get shepherding from a pastor, which the Bible says is critical to spiritual development. Think of how you can use what you are doing on campus to build and support your local congregation. Invite others from campus to church with you. Think about it. After you have graduated and potentially moved away from school, that church will most likely still be there. You can ensure that future students have a place of worship. You are not only a luminary for Christ, but also an emissary for your local church.

I have heard the argument that all that matters is that people come to Jesus. That is not completely true. Without that accountability and covering of a church body and a pastor, people are not set up for success spiritually. It's a commitment to Christ and commitment to the people of God that helps us find the healthy balance Jesus wanted us to have.

BEFORE
GRADUATING

Will it matter that you ever attended your school? I pray that the answer is yes. You only have a set amount of time that you will have this great opportunity for global impact. You must make the most of your college experience. Abandon thoughts of wild parties and countless drunken one night stands. That life will always bring death. You are Jesus Christ's ambassador on your campus, and you have a job to do. God has placed in you everything you need to leave an indelible print on your campus. Your job is to walk with the Holy Spirit as He leads you onward.

"But you are a chosen people, a royal priesthood,
a holy nation, a people belonging to God, that
you may declare the praises of him who called
you out of darkness into his wonderful light."

1 Peter 2:9 (NIV)

Remember it's not your responsibility to make people believe in Christ. You must declare His praises and greatness as loud as you can. This will take some strategy, insight, wisdom, and guidance. It's not an easy task that lies ahead of you but one you must complete. Use the resources you have at your fingertips. Only you and God know the relationships you've build and the chances around you for impact. You must and will have to answer to Him for how you stewarded your college years. This is not to induce guilt but rather to inspire movement.

Upon graduation you will wish you could have these moments again. You will run into people who you remember from school and wonder where they stand spiritually. Sadly, some will have come no closer; others will have slipped into eternity not knowing the Savior. This may feel like I am attempting to scare you into action, but no. This is the truth. It's the same truth that every Christian has to face. When Christ went to be with the Father, He gave us a job to do and that is making sure that we tell others about Him with our mouths and lives.

God has given you a mission field that is unique and can directly impact the entire world. This is not an over statement. Most people will never have the amount people from such diverse places as you have around you on campus right now.

Look around you. Listen to the varied accents you hear. The world is at your door step. People travel to the furthest reaches of the globe to be educated. Is it beyond the realm of possibility that God allowed them to go to your school so you would be able to tell them about Christ? Those same people are in your classrooms, your dorms, and your study groups everyday.

I was discussing this with my wife recently, and we were reminiscing over our college years. We talked about the friendships we established and the crazy things we did to touch lives on campus. We remembered one time specifically when the campus was closed in observance of Thanksgiving (which is uniquely an American holiday). Many international students were stuck on campus. So, we had an international Thanksgiving dinner where we fed students from abroad and shared our faith. I have no idea where those people are now, but they have heard the message. We touched the lives of people that are now in countries we may never visit, but our impact did.

College should be the most exciting time of your life. You can experiment with who you are and who you think you're called to be without anyone even looking at you strange. It's included in the college experience. You can find your God given talents and use them for His glory. You can just act like a big kid, and it is perfectly fine! College is great! There is no other time in your life that you will have such freedom and opportunities. I encourage you to live it up, for Christ.

Can you imagine what your campus would be like if everyone would yield to the gospel message? How would it feel? What if there was the sense that God was present? How would people respond? This is the kind of thought that I pray wakes you up at night. You have to start believing that God wants to do something great through you on your campus.

You have to try. Take a chance. In your own way, whether big or small, take a step today to increase the knowledge of Christ on your campus. Pray radical prayers that shake the very foundations of those around you. Befriend the oddest of people for the sake of the cross. All heaven is cheering you on.

It's not enough to just be called a Christian and do nothing. Show your faith by your works. I talk often students who ask me what they can do. My question back to them is, "What can't you do?" The possibilities are as limitless as your imagination. The challenge is that we can become unaccustomed to thinking creatively as it pertains to our own impact. You are intelligent and able to do more through Christ than you can even imagine. God has entrusted you with your campus for as long as you are there.

Don't Be In a Rush

One of my pet peeves as a college minister is when students are so busy trying to get out of college that they miss the college experience. Sometimes we can be so focused on "growing up" that we squander the chances we have to maximize where we are. Life is coming for you; you don't have to worry about that. Get your education; work your part- or full-time job. Embrace internship opportunities that come your way. But, don't be so focused on the adult life that you miss the college life. Of course, this doesn't include non-traditional students who are actually older adults with other constraints.

You may want to consider holding off on getting married. This is not a requirement, but rather a thought. If marriage will distract you from impacting those around you, then it may be worth it to wait. All I am saying is that advancing the Kingdom of God is of the utmost importance. I married my wife within a year of graduating from college. We would have considered getting married sooner, but our pastor encouraged us to finish school first. It was the best advice for us because we both wanted to finish strong.

You may have a lot of older friends that are into living their single lives. Enjoy your time with them, but don't be in such a hurry to be like them that you stop engaging in the lives of those at school. Serve at your local church with all you have, but make sure there is some fruit from your service on campus. Make college count!

Closing Remarks

I hope in some way this book has inspired you to pour your life into relevant ministry on your campus. I believe that if we can win the campuses in this country alone to Christ, we can change the world. My prayer is that college Christians from around the world would fall passionately in love with Christ and leverage their lives for God where they are. Who knows... the next major move of God could come from the campuses.

That is why I have served in college ministry for so many years. I believe inherent within every college believer there is the ability to lead. The very fact that Jesus calls us light to a dark world says that we as Christians are to guide people out of darkness. There is a great need for light on today's college campuses, and I believe that Christ's followers are the answer. You must lead people to the One who can satisfy their greatest need. You need to only choose to shine. If you would leverage your life for Christ's sake on your campus, you just may change the world.

Appendix A

Incoming Freshmen

It can be both scary and exciting to enter a college campus for the first time. I encourage any first year students to prepare before entering the campus the first time. Spend time praying and asking God to help you see where you can make the greatest difference. Most people wait until they're well into their college years to even approach that question, if ever. If you enter school with a sense of direction, it will give you an advantage over other in coming students, both Christian and non-Christian alike.

You don't have to wait until you are an upper classman to impact your campus. So many Christians touch down on the school grounds and wait for something to happen. Don't wait! Jump right in. Do your research. Before you get there, see what the campus has to offer. See if there are organizations that do what you are interested in. Find out the major needs of the campus and see if you have what it takes to meet one of those needs. If you take the offense you may be surprised as to the difference you can make relatively quickly.

You must be like the children and spy out the land.

"Then Moses sent them to spy out the land of Canaan, and said to them, "Go up this *way* into the South, and go up to the mountains, and see what the land is like: whether the people who dwell in it *are* strong or weak, few or many; whether the land they dwell in *is* good or bad; whether the cities they inhabit *are* like camps or strongholds; whether the land *is* rich or poor; and whether there are forests there or not. Be of good courage..."

Numbers 13:17–20

The better you understand the school you are going to attend the more prepared you will be to touch the lives of the others. Don't enter as a lamb to the slaughter; go in savvy as a senior. Other freshman will gravitate to you based on that alone.

Caution: There are so many people who will encourage you to, "have fun", or "get some experiences", this is a nice way to say fill up on the sin side of the "college experience".

I hear people say these things to college first years all the time, and it is one of the scariest bits of advice I have ever heard. Here is why, you never know what "experience" will be your last. You never know what "experience" will be your gateway to more dangerous living. Lastly, you don't know what "experience" could lead you far away from Christ. That is the largest and most concerning issue, the love of God could become a distant thought.

I believe you should make the most of your campus life, but the Holy Spirit should guide those times. Trust me, if you commit to living for Christ with all of your mind, heart and strength you will have an "experience" of a lifetime. Make your college years count eternally.

Appendix B

Christian Campuses

Christian schools serve very important purposes. I understand the need for Christian education and instruction. Especially, when preparing to enter a ministry based career. I see a problem with getting biblical instructions from people who don't embrace the Bible themselves. That increases the chances for incorrect teaching, which can confuse some and derail others. So yes, schools that are Christ centered are good and helpful.

There is an inherent issue that occasionally occurs. Students can sometimes begin to think that the Christian campus is the world. The world outside of the campus walls is very different. You see when most of the people you are around agree with you, and then you can develop lack of desire to evangelize. Why, because you don't have reminders around you of lost people. Now, some Christian schools do a very good job of encouraging students to go into the surrounding communities and touching them with the love of God. But, not all schools have that component. If that is the case at your school, you may have to challenge the culture.

There should also be no assumptions that all the students on the campus are believers. I remember visiting a Christian campus in Chicago, where they were having a religious emphasis week. We communicated the Gospel, and at the end of the night gave an invitation to Christ. And there were numbers of students who responded. There were people on that campus that were church group kids that never responded to Jesus. Others were from other countries and just coming here to go to school. One girl was from a traditional Muslim family, and she came to Christ and had to figure out how to tell them. There are people that need Jesus around you even on a spiritually aware campus.

Going to chapel service does not a Christian make. Even on the most amazing campuses there are people you can reach. Think about those from the community who work at the school in the cafeteria, or in maintenance, etc. Don't miss the opportunities around you, and if everyone is saved then look to the community. You may be the catalyst for your entire campus to serve the community more effectively. Even on at a Christian school you can accomplish the great commission.

Appendix C

Church Leaders

My hope and prayers for you as a church leader is that you would allow God to touch your heart in the area of college ministry. If you have a population of college students or young adults anywhere near you, I urge you to seriously consider making them a focus. Think about it. Most churches have a population of children through high school and there is a large gap that picks up around 30 or 40 years of age. This is a growing issue in churches across the country. Churches are losing the next generation. What that means is that your church's lifespan has just been set. If you can't keep your church filled with young adults then your church will die in the next 30 years.

Think about it, one of the challenges many churches face is know how to communicate to the next generation. That starts with having people in your congregation that are from that generation and give them a voice in your planning. They can express the needs of their peers and help your church meet the needs of their population. That will not only make your church relevant, but you will increase your churches lifespan, because you always have the next group of church leaders coming forward.

There is also a direct financial component. I don't know of a church that doesn't need more commitment in the area of tithes and offerings. I didn't learn how to give as an adult with my finances already leveraged. It takes a lot more effort to convince someone who has a lot to lose to tithe money they already have committed. But, if you reach a young adult who makes roughly $13, 000 a year to tithe on the little they make then you give them a principle to follow when they have 40k, 50k, and more. I learned to tithe early and now it is not an option, it's a way of life. What church leader doesn't want that.

The reality is, the church needs money to function and these young people will brings funds that will be necessary in the next 4–6 years. If you effectively impact young adults you could get rid of all capital raising campaigns. This is just something to consider. Not to mention that there is a generation of young adults that may never come to a life filled with the love and glory of God if they are not reaching during this window of life. I could say more, but I pray that God touches your heart with a passion for the 18–25 year old population around you.

Appendix D

Youth Ministry Leaders

You are on the front lines. As a college ministry leader I want to encourage you to see your students as kingdom agents on their high school campuses. Then they may fare better as young adults. So many freshmen have no clue as to how to stand firm on college campuses. It's your responsibility to prepare them to not just try to stay away from sin but to excel as Christians. You can't settle for being a glorified baby sitter. Not that you see yourself as one, but some churches and parents are happy to have their children occupied. This is a different perspective from seeing them as missionaries.

It has to break your heart that when your students go to college and walk away from a relationship with Christ. I can't imagine anything more frustrating then pouring your life into kids to see them abandon it all. So I want to encourage you to help them fully understand their faith, and how to defend it apologetically. Not apologizing for it.

Challenge them to live out loud right where they are. Our local high school pastor is amazing at it, and his value to our church is high. For example, in order to get to get baptized he makes students where a 10 inch cross for an entire week, and explain the gospel to everyone who asks. Which means that he fully teaches them the gospel. That is the kind of challenge many high school students need. That looks a lot like the early church; you had to be fully identified as a Christian before you were considered one.

Please make sure you students don't just see our faith as a moral movement. Make sure that they see the glory of God as the most important thing in their lives. Tell of the challenges they will face on the college campus. Make sure you prepare them to tell their testimony. The future is in your hands and I pray that you manage it well. I pray you don't loose one more student to the "college experience".

Appendix E

College Pastors

To my fellow college pastors I have one main request, stay. So many people are serving as college pastors that are just looking for the next big opportunity. College ministry should not be the holding ground for people who want to be senior pastors. Becoming a senior pastor is a good goal, but not at the expense of your students. So, again please stay where you are as long as God will allow.

It should be the goal of college leaders to stay still long enough to see two generations of students come through your ministry. That means staying for at least two cycles of students to go from freshmen through their senior years. This is a big commitment but your students deserve that much. Imagine the testimony of a student excited about working with you because they remember the impact you had on their older sibling. Now, imagine how disappointed a student is when they have 2–3 college pastors over the course of their college career. It's hard to leave any kind of imprint on a student or a campus when you have not proven your commitment to either, because you are in such a rush to get to other pursuits.

Once again I am a college pastor and I have had my share of disappointment and failure. But, over time my investments in students and campuses in my area have yielded a return on the investment. College ministry can be very difficult as your churches or organization's leadership can misunderstand you. It is often the least funded area and there are many people who see it as a waste of time and attention. I make this promise to you, if you stay still and give your all to college ministry, it will be more than worth it. I pray that you will ever be encouraged. It's a good work!

About the Author

Damian Boyd, Sr. is a committed follower of Jesus Christ, passionate communicator, and visionary leader. For more than thirteen years, he has reached and developed youth, college students, young adults, and singles locally and nationally through personal ministry, conferences, high impact training events, programs, and leadership gatherings. His life mission is to lead, train, and develop people with the principles, tools, and resources to live significant lives for the Glory of God. His life scripture continues to be the theme of his life and ministry. "You are the salt of the earth…You are the light of the world…" (Matthew 5:13–15).

Damian currently serves as a staff member at Destiny Metropolitan Worship Church in Atlanta, Georgia, where he is the College and Young Professionals Ministry Director. He is known for his creativity, strategic thinking, and down-to-earth yet challenging communication style. He along with his wife, Zarat, and son, Damian Jr., live in Marietta, Georgia.

For booking information and resources
from the author, please visit
www.damianlboyd.com

LaVergne, TN USA
30 July 2010
191411LV00004B/22/P